ALSO BY JON WINOKUR

ENNUI
TO GO

THE
ART
OF
BORE-
DOM

Compiled & Edited by
JON WINOKUR
Author of **THE PORTABLE CURMUDGEON**

SASQUATCH BOOKS
SEATTLE

Printed in Canada
Published by Sasquatch Books
Distributed by Publishers Group West
13 12 11 10 09 08 07 06 05   6 5 4 3 2 1

Cover illustration: Greg Clarke
Book design: Kate Basart/Union Pageworks

Library of Congress Cataloging-in-Publication Data
Ennui to go / [collected] by Jon Winokur
          p. cm.
          Includes bibliographical references and index.
          ISBN 1-57061-444-X
          1. Boredom—Quotations, maxims, etc. I. Winokur, Jon.

PN6084.B66E55 2005
152.4—dc22   2005042559

Sasquatch Books | 119 South Main Street, Ste 400
Seattle, WA 98104 | 206/467-4300
www.sasquatchbooks.com | custserv@sasquatchbooks.com

For TB: curmudgeon, co-religionist, boredom buster

ENNUI (ahn **wee**) *noun*: intense boredom;
a state of mental weariness and discontent
resulting from lack of interest.

CONTENTS

ACKNOWLEDGMENTS

I wish to thank Peter Bell, Reid Boates, Norrie Epstein, Léna Lagorce, Gary Luke, Al Rasof, and Elinor Winokur for their invaluable contributions to this book.

The basic fact about human existence is not that it is a tragedy, but that it is a bore. It is not so much a war as an endless standing in line.

H. L. MENCKEN

So little time, so little to do.

OSCAR LEVANT

INTRODUCTION

Though boredom is commonly deemed trivial, it ranks with war, revolution, and economic upheaval as a force in human affairs. Bertrand Russell called it "one of the great motive powers throughout the historical epoch." The sociologist Robert Nisbet identified it as one of the most "insistent and universal" of the factors influencing human behavior. The astronomer Harlow Shapley included boredom with nuclear war, global warming, and overpopulation as potential causes of the end of civilization. Kierkegaard saw boredom as "the root of all evil," and according to Saul Bellow, "the two real problems in life are boredom and death."

Boredom began as a luxury. For most of human history people were too busy trying to survive to be bored, but by the eighteenth century the rich suddenly had the leisure to worry about whether they were having fun, and boredom has flourished ever since. Epidemic boredom is one of postmillennial America's dirtiest little secrets, and a contributing cause of our national malaise. Why are we so bored? In part because modern technology showers us in an endless stream of sensations, shrinking attention spans and lowering boredom thresholds. Television, for example, portrays a fantasy world that makes real life seem boring by comparison. It creates the expectation that *everything* should be entertaining—a notion especially prevalent among children, who expect to be amused everywhere, including at school. TV news comes at us in smaller and smaller bites and increasingly vivid images, reducing complex issues to a few seconds of dramatic video. And then there's the remote control.

But it isn't just television. The entertainment choices are virtually unlimited. With the Internet, computer games, CDs, DVDs, web-surfing-computer-game-playing-digital-photo-taking cell phones, there's more and more to do than ever before, but, paradoxically, less and less worth doing. The more we're entertained, the more we're bored, because we now assume that life owes us a good time.

"Life, friends, is boring. We must not say so," wrote the poet John Berryman, and being bored has long been regarded as a personal failing. Samuel Butler admonished that "the man who lets himself be bored is even more contemptible than the bore." Thomas Jefferson cautioned his daughter that "it is our own fault if we ever know what ennui is," and mothers everywhere still warn their children that "when you're bored you're boring." People will own up to all kinds of faults before they'll admit being bored. You're probably more likely to hear, "My name is Jason and I'm a cross-dressing clutterer" ("HELLO, JASON!") than, "My name is Jason and I'm bored." There's also the widespread notion that it's impolite to inflict our boredom on others, the way we're obliged not to cough in their faces or complain about our sciatica. (The title character of Anton Chekhov's *Ivanov* kills himself partly out of fear that he's a bore.)

Yet, the world is full of bores. What, precisely, is a bore? "A person who talks when you wish him to listen," according to Ambrose Bierce's *Devil's Dictionary*; "someone who tells everything" (Voltaire); "a man who is never unintentionally rude" (Oscar Wilde). Once, in his cups, Dylan Thomas suddenly looked up and said, "Somebody's boring me. I think it's me."

Nietzsche asked, "Is not life a hundred times too short for us to bore ourselves?" Well of course it is! Which makes existential ennui even more insufferable. But is it really our fault? Nietzsche also wrote that "against boredom even the gods themselves struggle in vain." Maybe some of us are predisposed to boredom, while others are born with a talent for keeping busy. These lucky people get so wrapped up in work or family or religion or hobbies that they rarely suffer boredom. For your congenital ennuyé, however, keeping busy is not an option. Most of us come down in the middle ground where, despite rare flashes of joy and excitement, life is just too dull to provide sustained engagement, and the innate need for novelty compels us to seek diversion. It can be stated as a simple equation: Free time, plus the need for novelty, minus novelty, equals ennui.

The fear of boredom can be more powerful than boredom itself. The annals of ennui are replete with examples of what Bertrand Russell called "the flight from boredom." Countless palliatives and supposed antidotes have been tried, many of them self-destructive. People have committed crimes, gambled away fortunes, engaged in litigation, sniffed glue, gotten married, fought duels, and mutilated themselves out of sheer boredom. (Another Chekov character says, "I'm so bored I could take a run at a wall!") Graham Greene once pretended to have an abscess so he could have a tooth pulled and thereby cheat ennui with a few minutes of ether-induced oblivion. A fifteen-year-old boy who raped and murdered a young woman told police that he and his friends selected their victim at random because they were bored: "There was nothing to do and so I guess we had the impression of going out in the field and kill somebody," he said. Many travel: The desire to flee the "exhausted sterilities of Western civilization" was how Kingsley Amis explained his frequent trips abroad. Others drink or take drugs or overeat. Sex is another refuge, as are less intimate forms of thrill seeking such as bungee jumping or "train surfing" (see *Las Surfistas*, page 157). But beware: Antidotes can also be inducers, as in the cases of games (page 143), travel (page 120) and, ironically, tips for beating boredom (page 117), which only seem to produce more of it.

On the other hand, boredom can be a great motivator, a stimulant as well as a depressant. It can trigger progress when the need for novelty spurs invention. Though ennuyés incline to angst, *weltschmerz,* rage, and nihilism, they also tend to be artists, innovators, and pioneers. Their boredom is their inspiration. They find sanctuary in the imagination, where they create a world for themselves that isn't boring. That's the good news: Under the right conditions, ennui engenders originality, often in the form of quotable quotations, which brings us to the delicate mission at hand: A book about boredom must be careful not to become what it beholds, so I hope *Ennui to Go* will demonstrate that boredom isn't necessarily boring, and that while boredom experienced is depressing, boredom considered can be fascinating. This book is intended as a balm for bored people everywhere, to be browsed on the bus, the subway, the plane, while waiting in line or waiting for Godot, to assuage the ennui of daily life sort of like the way Ritalin calms hyperactivity. If it is anodyne, maybe it's because the recognition of ennui—the acknowledgment that the reader is not alone in his or her boredom—is oddly encouraging. It should also make a swell gift for that hard-to-shop-for ennuyé who has everything except . . . interests. So, ennui sufferers unite! You have nothing to lose but the blahs.

—J. W., JANUARY 2005

USAGE NOTE

The French *ennui,* which entered the English language in the late seventeenth century, derives from an Old French word for annoyance, and before that from *odium,* Latin for hatred or dislike. It's probably no accident that ennui is French—the Gauls are especially susceptible to it and particularly eloquent in describing its discontents (see page 57 for a list of ennui-related Gallicisms). The English, on the other hand, invented the idea of "boredom": The first recorded use of the word was in 1768, by Earle Carlisle, who used it, as it happened, to insult a Frenchman.

In her book, *Boredom: The Literary History of a State of Mind,* Patricia Meyer Spacks notes that the concept of boredom arose with "the emergence of leisure, the decline of orthodox Christianity" and "the newly elaborated notion of individual rights"—including the right to be bored. She traces a gradual shift from blaming boredom on the victim to ascribing it to external conditions, a change from a "moralistic" to a "sociological" view:

Boredom was not (*is* not) the same as ennui, more closely related to acedia. Ennui implies a judgment of the universe; boredom, a response to the immediate. Ennui belongs to those with a sense of sublime potential, those who feel themselves superior to their environment.

In other words, if an Englishman was bored it was because of circumstances, but if a Frenchman had ennui it was his own fault.

Other distinctions have been suggested: Ennui is a disease, boredom a symptom. Or it's a question of degree: Ennui lasts longer and goes deeper than boredom, hence boredom is to ennui what sadness is to clinical depression, the former acute, the latter chronic. Or boredom is passive, ennui active. It has even been suggested that "the poor get bored but the rich have ennui." Still, most English language dictionaries treat "ennui" and "boredom" as equivalent. *Webster's Third New International Dictionary* (1971) is typical: Ennui is "a feeling of weariness and dissatisfaction : languor or emptiness of spirit : tedium, boredom"; boredom is "the state of being bored : ennui." In practice the two terms are also used synonymously: When English speakers say one they often mean the other. This book likewise uses them interchangeably.

For what it's worth, I tend to think of boredom/ennui as the absence of what psychologist Mihaly Csikszentmihalyi calls "flow," the complete engagement in some activity, the undivided, self-forgetting attention we give to something in which we have an intense interest. By that measure, I'd have to admit that I'm bored much of the time. How about you?

ANATOMY
OF ENNUI

Among the forces that have shaped human behavior boredom is one of the most insistent and universal. Although scarcely as measurable a factor in history as war, disease, economic depression, famine, and revolution, it is far from invisible in either the present or the past. A stream of chronicles, diaries, memoirs, and biographies yields much information on attacks of boredom and their consequences as well as on antidotes or preventives. Suetonius, Petronius Arbiter, Robert Burton, Saint-Simon at the Court of Louis xiv, and the Marquis de Sade are among those who left observations, reflections, and analyses of boredom. The range of cures or terminations of boredom is a wide one: migration, desertion, war, revolution, murder, calculated cruelty to others, suicide, pornography, alcohol, narcotics. Whether it is Tiberius relishing those he tortured, or Sherlock Holmes taking to the needle, the pains and the results

of boredom are everywhere to be seen,
and nowhere more epidemically than in
Western society at the present time.

ROBERT NISBET

The effect of boredom on a large scale
in history is underestimated. It is a main
cause of revolutions, and would soon
bring to an end all the static Utopias and
the farmyard civilization of the Fabians.

WILLIAM RALPH INGE

The two enemies of human happiness are
pain and boredom.

ARTHUR SCHOPENHAUER

In human existence, the intervals
between pleasure and pain are occupied
by ennui. And since all pleasures are like

cobwebs, exceedingly fragile, thin, and transparent, ennui penetrates their tissue and saturates them, just as air penetrates the webs. It is, indeed, nothing but a yearning for happiness, without the illusion of pleasure or the reality of pain. This yearning is never satisfied, since true happiness does not exist. So that life is interwoven with weariness and suffering, and one of these evils disappears only to give place to the other. Such is the destiny of man.

GIACOMO LEOPARDI

Ennui has made more gamblers than avarice, more drunkards than thirst, and perhaps as many suicides as despair.

C. C. COLTON

Boredom: A state of instinctual tension in which the instinctual aims are repressed but in which the tension as such is felt; and therefore one turns to the external world for help in the struggle against repression. The person who is bored can be compared to someone who has forgotten a name and inquires about it from others.

OTTO FENICHEL

There is a strange haziness about the state commonly referred to as boredom. While the literature on it is quite limited, it nonetheless *has* one (most of it recent), unlike other states of mind such as joy, envy, or fear, and a literature moreover much of which is concerned not simply to describe its origins, operations and effects, but to determine just what it actually *is*. What emerges is the rather puzzling fact that, again unlike other mental states, boredom has a complex and enigmatic past, and an ambiguous present. While it is generally paid scant and superficial attention, passed over lightly as transitory and insignificant, the ready-made phrases of the language seem to tell a different tale: "bored to tears," "bored stiff," "bored silly," "bored to death," and, more recently, "bored out of one's skull."

Seán Desmond Healy

Boredom is the loss of the capacity to wonder, to appreciate the sense of mystery and awe in life.

Rollo May

Boredom is one of the ways we break our habit of believing in the future. When there's nothing we want, nothing to look forward to, the story stops.

ADAM PHILLIPS

Boredom is an emptiness filled with insistence.

LEO STEIN

Boredom flourishes . . . when you feel safe. It's a symptom of security.

EUGENE IONESCO

Boredom is the feeling that everything is a waste of time; serenity, that nothing is.

THOMAS SZASZ

If sleep is the apogee of physical relaxation, boredom is the apogee of mental relaxation. Boredom is the dream bird that hatches the egg of experience. A rustling in the leaves drives him away.

WALTER BENJAMIN

Boredom is relative. One can find great joy and fulfillment in a long afternoon of porch sitting. One can be bored at the task of skydiving or rock climbing. It's what is in the mind that counts.

HANS ZEIGER

Boredom is like a pitiless zooming in on the epidermis of time. Every instant is dilated and magnified like the pores of the face.

JEAN BAUDRILLARD

Boredom is rage spread thin.

PAUL TILLICH

Boredom is one face of death.

JULIEN GREEN

Is boredom anything less than the sense
of one's faculties slowly dying?

JOHN BERGER

The desire for desires.

LEO TOLSTOY

Psychic anorexia.

SEÁN DESMOND HEALY

You'll find boredom where there is an absence of a good idea.

EARL NIGHTINGALE

The word "boredom" did not even exist until the eighteenth century. In an agricultural society in which you were struggling to stay alive, you had no time to be bored. You worked, you slept, and you worked again. Life was expected to be hard. Reading by the fire or playing checkers at the general store were great luxuries. If you were affected by "ennui," it was presumed to be your own fault, even a sin. "Idle hands are the devil's playthings," pioneer preachers warned.

SHARON LINNÉA

Eighteenth-century thinkers associate boredom unambiguously with moral failure. Its remedy involves mental, moral, or spiritual discipline. Nineteenth-century commentators connect it with class arrogance, with inadequate responsiveness to others, sometimes with capitalistic false value. They too frequently imply that it can be remedied by self-discipline.

PATRICIA MEYER SPACKS

Boredom, after all, is a form of criticism.

WILLIAM PHILLIPS

Tedium, n. Ennui, the state or condition of one that is bored. Many fanciful derivations of the word have been affirmed, but so high an authority as Father Jape says that it comes from a very obvious source—the first words of the ancient Latin hymn *Te Deum Laudamus*. In this apparently natural derivation there is something that saddens.

AMBROSE BIERCE

For thinkers and all sensitive spirits, boredom is that disagreeable "windless calm" of the soul that precedes a happy voyage and cheerful winds. They have to bear it and must wait for its effect on them. Precisely this is what lesser nature cannot achieve by any means.

FRIEDRICH WILHELM NIETZSCHE

Boredom is the most horrible of wolves.

JEAN GIONO

Full of ennui—that is to say, empty.

VICTOR HUGO

Yet if she felt anything it was ennui
. . . the grey sky and the cold wind
obliterating every impulse she might
have felt to seek comfort in another
climate, another landscape. She was free
to leave but felt condemned to stay.

ANITA BROOKNER

Man is the only animal that can be *bored*.

ERICH FROMM

Man is bored not only when there is nothing to do, but also when there is too much, or when everything waiting to be done has lost its luster.

GEOFFREY CLIVE

One receives as reward for much ennui, despondency, boredom—such as a solitude without friends, books, duties, passions must bring with it— those quarter-hours of profoundest contemplation within oneself and nature. He who completely entrenches himself against boredom also entrenches himself against himself: he will never get to drink the strongest refreshing draught from his own innermost fountain.

FRIEDRICH WILHELM NIETZSCHE

Boredom can be very useful, say its friends. Great inventions have come along because the inventor was bored with his life and casting about for solutions. Romances have resulted because young lovers had experienced boredom with somebody less interesting and were driven to link up with a non-boring person.

Celestine Sibley

[Boredom is] the great enemy of the modern world . . . perhaps the underlying cause of all our troubles.

Pierre Teilhard de Chardin

My story is much too sad to be told,
But practically everything leaves me totally cold.

The only exception I know is the case
When I'm out on a quiet spree
Fighting vainly the old ennui. . . .

COLE PORTER

The "old ennui," after all, is one of our
most insidious opponents in life. It lacks
the medical authenticity of depression,
and it possesses none of that Melvillean
grandeur we associate with "damp, dark
Novembers in the soul." Still, boredom
(ennui sounds so much more fashionable)
gets its grip on all of us with varying
degrees of frequency, and there is no
immunity.

BILL OTT

Boredom has become an embracing
rubric of discontent.

PATRICIA MEYER SPACKS

Boredom depends on the nothingness
that pervades reality; it causes a dizziness
like that produced by looking down into
a yawning chasm.

SOREN KIERKEGAARD

The war between being and nothingness
is the underlying illness of the twentieth
century. Boredom slays more of
existence than war.

NORMAN MAILER

This Ennui, for which we Saxons had
no name, this word of France has got a
terrific significance. It shortens life, and
bereaves the day of its light.

RALPH WALDO EMERSON

Grasp your opportunities, no matter how poor your health; *nothing* is worse for your health than boredom.

Mignon McLaughlin

Boredom is always counter-revolutionary.

Guy Debord

The world is eaten up by boredom. . . . It is like dust. You go about and never notice. . . . But stand still for an instant and there it is, coating your face and hands.

George Bernanos

What made me suffer was not so much boredom itself as the idea that I could, and should, *not* be bored. I also belonged to a noble and very ancient family which had never been bored, which had always had a direct and concrete relationship with reality. I had to forget this family and to accept, once and for all, the position in which I found myself. But could one live in a state of boredom, could one live without any relationship with anything real, and not suffer from it? Here was the whole problem.

ALBERTO MORAVIA

It is not the simple statement of facts that ushers in freedom; it is the constant repetition of them that has this liberating effect. Tolerance is the result not of enlightenment, but of boredom.

QUENTIN CRISP

Boredom is the root of all evil. Strange that boredom, in itself so staid and stolid, should have such power to set in motion. The influence it exerts is altogether magical, except that it is not the influence of attraction, but of repulsion. . . . Since boredom advances and boredom is the root of all evil, no wonder, then, that the world goes backwards, that evil spreads. This can be traced back to the very beginning of the world. The gods were bored; therefore they created human beings.

SØREN KIERKEGAARD

Boredom is an evil that is not to be estimated lightly. It can come in the end to real despair. The public authority takes precautions against it everywhere, as against other universal calamities.

ARTHUR SCHOPENHAUER

Owen's boredom meant that he had a limited attention span: he always needed new people to break what he experienced as the monotony of the old.

ANITA BROOKNER

Things have dropped from me. I have outlived certain desires; I have lost friends, some by death . . . others through sheer inability to cross the street.

VIRGINIA WOOLF

Indifference expanding to Ennui
Takes on the feel of Immortality

CHARLES BAUDELAIRE

Ennui, felt on the proper occasions, is a sign of intelligence.

CLIFTON FADIMAN

Boredom speaks the language of time, and it teaches you the most valuable lesson of your life: the lesson of your utter insignificance.

JOSEPH BRODSKY

The tedium is the message.

BRIAN ENO

Perhaps this quiet yet unquiet waiting is the harbinger of grace, or perhaps it is grace itself.

FRANZ KAFKA

THE BORED AND THE BORING

Society is now one polish'd horde,
Form'd of two mighty tribes, the *Bores*
and *Bored*.

LORD BYRON

Perhaps the world's second worst crime
is boredom. The first is being a bore.

CECIL BEATON

The secret of being a bore is to tell
everything.

VOLTAIRE

Bores can be divided into two classes:
those who have their own particular
subject, and those who do not need a
subject.

A. A. MILNE

Bore: a man who is never unintentionally rude.

Oscar Wilde

Plato was a bore.

Friedrich Wilhelm Nietzsche

The man who lets himself be bored is even more contemptible than the bore.

Samuel Butler

I can't remember being bored, not once in my whole life.

Harry S Truman

What's wrong with being a boring kind of guy?

GEORGE H. W. BUSH

Life is never boring, but some people choose to be bored.

WAYNE DYER

It is the peculiarity of the bore that he is the last person to find himself out.

OLIVER WENDELL HOLMES, SR.

He is not only dull himself, he is the cause of dullness in others.

SAMUEL FOOTE

His shortcoming is his long staying.

LEWIS L. LEWISOHN

He's the kind of bore who's here today and here tomorrow.

BINNIE BARNES

He is not only a bore, but he bores for England.

MALCOLM MUGGERIDGE
(said of Anthony Eden)

Bores bore each other too, but it never seems to teach them anything.

DON MARQUIS

It is very difficult to delineate a bore in a narrative, for the simple reason that he is a bore. A tale must aim at condensation, but a bore acts in solution. It is only in the long run that he is ascertained.

JOHN HENRY CARDINAL NEWMAN

We often forgive those who bore us, but we cannot forgive those whom we bore.

LA ROCHEFOUCAULD

You must be careful about giving any drink whatsoever to a bore. A lit-up bore is the worst in the world.

DAVID CECIL

A bore is a fellow talking who can change the subject back to his topic of conversation faster than you can change it back to yours.

LAURENCE J. PETER

A bore is a man who has nothing to say and says it anyway.

BERT TAYLOR

The merely well-informed man is the most useless bore on God's earth.

ALFRED NORTH WHITEHEAD

Bore: a man who deprives you of solitude without providing you with company.

GIAN VICENZO GRAVINA

A bore is someone who persists in holding his own views after we have enlightened him with ours.

MALCOLM FORBES

If at first you do succeed, try, try not to be a bore.

FRANKLIN P. JONES

A bore is a guy who wraps up a two-minute idea in a two-hour vocabulary.

WALTER WINCHELL

There are more bores around than when I was a boy.

FRED ALLEN

As I usually do when I want to get rid of someone whose conversation bores me, I pretended to agree.

ALBERT CAMUS

It's so much easier to pray for a bore than to go and see one.

C. S. LEWIS

The worst sin in politics is being boring.

RICHARD M. NIXON

[McGeorge] Bundy and [John Fitzgerald] Kennedy got on well from the start, both were quick and bright, both hating to be

bored and to bore; that was almost
the worst offense a man could commit,
to bore.

DAVID HALBERSTAM

The nice thing about being a celebrity is
that when you bore people, they think
it's their fault.

HENRY KISSINGER

I am one of those unhappy persons who
inspires bores to the highest flights of art.

EDITH SITWELL

Every improvement in communication
makes the bore more terrible.

FRANK MOORE COLBY

Highly educated bores are by far the worst: They know so much, in such fiendish detail, to be boring about.

LOUIS KRONENBERGER

The world is a difficult world indeed
And people are hard to suit
And the man who plays the violin
Is a bore to the man with a flute.

SIR THOMAS BEECHAM

A lot of self-help books wind up looking for euphemistic ways to help people cope with the fact that they are bored and/or boring.

COLIN MCENROE

Every hero becomes a bore at last.

Ralph Waldo Emerson

Everybody is somebody's bore.

Edith Sitwell

The age of chivalry is past. Bores have succeeded to dragons.

Benjamin Disraeli

From every Englishman emanates a kind of gas, the deadly chokedamp of boredom.

Heinrich Heine

One out of three hundred and twelve Americans is a bore . . . and a healthy male adult bore consumes *each year* one and a half times his own weight in other people's patience.

JOHN UPDIKE

I am quite serious when I say that I do not believe there are, on the whole earth besides, so many intensified bores as in these United States. No man can form an adequate idea of the real meaning of the word, without coming here.

CHARLES DICKENS

In the U.S. you have to be a deviant or die of boredom.

WILLIAM S. BURROUGHS

LEXICON

acedia

Spiritual torpor, the scourge of medieval monks, who prayed so much that prayer began to bore them, which made them feel guilty, which in turn made boredom a sin.

There is a name for the generic shoulder shrug—the buzzing indifference, as if it's always 90 degrees in the shade after a large lunch. The word is acedia. It is the weariness of effort that extends to the heart and becomes a weariness of caring.

MELVIN MADDOCKS

acute boredom intolerance

Term coined by columnist Katherine A. Powers to describe the ennui generated by American media:

Of all the disabilities that are catered to in this great country of ours, one of them, I feel sure, never will be: acute boredom intolerance. It is crippling,

and the pathogens that trigger it are
spewed from every media orifice.
Just the mention of the presidential
campaign looming ahead has already sent
countless ABI victims into tailspins that
no amount of alcohol or antipsychotic
drugs can reverse. I know this because
I am afflicted, so severely in fact that I
was unable to attend my elder son's high
school graduation. Needless to say, I
cannot go to school plays or to the sports
events my other son gets himself involved
in. If either boy gets married, I hope he
elopes. When people talk of "panels,"
"performances," and "a chance to mingle,"
I have to leave the room. Beyond
this, I can scarcely enter a museum;
cannot go to readings under any
circumstances; and the word "theater"
induces acute respiratory distress.

When I speak of boredom I am not
talking about a response to the lack
of something, but rather to the suf-
focating presence of what the German

sociologist Georg Simmel called (in translation) "objective Geist." Too much spirit realized in the concrete; too much touching all the bases, examining the issues, and addressing concerns; too many memorable moments; too much sincerity; too much entertainment: too, too much and way too long.

adolescent torpor
Hormone-induced ennui. See also bor-ring!

apathy
Complete lack of interest or passion.

Most human beings have an infinite capacity for taking things for granted.

ALDOUS HUXLEY

Hate is not the opposite of love; apathy is.

ROLLO MAY

boredom boom

According to a Yankelovich survey conducted in 2000, a paradox exists whereby Americans are bored despite living in momentous times, evidently having developed tolerance to remarkable events the way drug users need increased doses to achieve the same high.

bored to death

Not just a figure of speech: see terminal ennui.

bor-ring!

Typical teenage reaction to virtually everything.

Is it not, indeed revealing, what the child's boredom evokes in adults? Heard as a demand, sometimes as an accusation of failure or disappointment, it is rarely agreed to, simply acknowledged. How often, in fact, the child's boredom is met by that most perplexing form of disapproval, the adult's wish to distract him—as though the adults have decided that the child's life must be, or be seen to be, endlessly interesting. It is one of the most oppressive demands of adults that the child should be interested, rather than take time to find what interests him.

ADAM PHILLIPS

cabin fever

Intense boredom caused by confinement indoors during long winters, which can result in infanticide, patricide, matricide, etc.

It's cabin fever season people, that time of year when four walls feel like they're going to come in here and choke the spirit right out of you. Time to lock away those firearms and hang tough. No way through it except to do it.

JEFF MELVOIN

curb-kicking time

Deliberately unstructured time (i.e., with no planned activities, television, or video games). See also downtime, healthy boredom.

Often, when children complain that they are bored, all they want is for a busy parent to stop and sit and talk for a while. They want attention and relationship. Other times, of course, it is good for children to experience boredom long enough to prompt them to find their own activity and stimulate their creativity.

RICHARD WINTER

downtime

A period of inactivity that can stimulate activity and recharge creative batteries. See also curb-kicking time, healthy boredom.

How boring it was. Of course, it was the making of me as a human being and a writer. Downtime is where we become ourselves, looking into the middle distance, kicking at the curb, lying on the grass or sitting on the stoop and staring at the tedious blue of the summer sky. I don't believe you can write poetry, or compose music, or become an actor without downtime, and plenty of it, a hiatus that passes for boredom but is really the quiet moving of the wheels inside that fuels creativity. And that to me is one of the saddest things about the lives of American children today. Soccer leagues, acting classes, tutors . . . our children are as overscheduled as we are, and that is saying something.

ANNA QUINDLEN

existential vacuum

State of boredom, inertia and apathy arising from a meaningless life, a concept posited by the psychotherapist and philosopher Viktor Frankl (1905–1997):

Patients complain of what they call an "inner void," and that is the reason why I have termed this condition the "existential vacuum." In contradistinction to the peak-experience so aptly described by Maslow, one could conceive of the existential vacuum in terms of an "abyss-experience."

fame-induced apathy

According to Douglas Coupland, "the attitude that no activity is worth pursuing unless one can become very famous pursuing it."

fatigue

Suffix added to describe boredom caused by overexposure to something, hence: "At the end of a full day at the Louvre, he was suffering from museum-fatigue"; "after watching TV with her husband, she had a bad case of football-fatigue"; "the American public suffers scandal-fatigue / campaign-fatigue / compassion-fatigue," etc.

flow

Rare state postulated by psychologist Mihaly Csikszentmihalyi in which people are completely absorbed in an activity, using their abilities to the utmost, losing all sense of time, experiencing satisfaction, perhaps even fulfillment:

Flow is generally reported when a person is doing his or her favorite activity—gardening, listening to music, bowling, cooking a good meal. It also occurs when driving, when talking to friends, and surprisingly often at work. Very rarely do people report flow in passive leisure activities, such as watching television or relaxing.

frigidaze
Zombie-like state of mindlessly peering into the refrigerator not out of hunger, but out of boredom.

healthy boredom
In the view of some child psychologists, boredom that leads to the development of creative and problem-solving skills. See also curb-kicking time, downtime.

instant gratification
Immediate pleasure or satisfaction.

Instant gratification takes too long.

CARRIE FISHER

languishing

A term coined by psychologist Paul Pearsall to describe the condition of being "hectically busy but chronically distracted, empty, disconnected, and unfulfilled."

mall ennui

The unique boredom induced by antiseptic, climate-controlled, Muzak-ed shopping malls, all of which seem to have the same stores (with names like Funk Station and Hot Topic).

la noia

Ennui, Italian style. Though untranslatable, roughly equivalent to boredom or ennui, only deeper. The concept was formulated by the poet and philosopher Giacomo Leopardi (1798–1837) who defined it in Operette morali *(1827):*

It seems to me that *la noia* is of the nature of air, which fills up all the spaces between material things and all the voids in each one of them; and whenever a body changes its place and is not at once replaced by another, *la noia* at once comes in. So all the intervals in human life between pleasure and pain, are occupied by *noia*. . . . Truly I believe that *la noia* means nothing more than a craving for pure happiness, unsatisfied by pleasure and not perceptibly wounded by wretchedness. And this craving . . . can never be gratified; so that true pleasure can never be found.

organized boredom of mass obedience

Criminologist Jeff Ferrell's term for the institutionalized boredom of daily life:

Under the dehumanizing conditions of modernism, boredom has come to pervade the experience of everyday life. This collective boredom has spawned

not only moments of illicit excitement—
that is, ephemeral crimes committed
against boredom itself—but larger
efflorescences of political and cultural
rebellion.

principle of maximum boredom
*Informal scientific axiom stating that the most
boring explanation is usually right.*

problem-solving deficit disorder
*Term coined by early childhood education
expert Diane Levin to describe the debilitating
effects on children of modern technology.
Countless hours being entertained in front of
television and computer screens creates the
expectation of instant gratification, prevents
children from developing their own creativity,
and may also lead to antisocial behavior.*

Life is boring when you haven't acquired
the capacity to solve problems as basic

as knowing how to fill your own time.
Why wouldn't that lead to acting-out
behaviors that get you labeled at school
and eventually even medicated?

SHARNA OLFMAN (CHILD PSYCHOLOGIST)

QFD
Quelle Fucking Drag.

Jamie got stuck at Rome airport for
thirty-six hours and it was, like, totally
QFD.

DOUGLAS COUPLAND

replayability
Industry jargon for the degree of novelty in a
video game based on such features as hidden
rooms and unexpected outcomes.

Every year, the players expect more and
more and more. If you came out now

with a game that looked like it was made
three years ago, they'd say it's boring.

RICK GIOLITO (VIDEO-GAME PRODUCER)

rustout
*Psychological exhaustion caused by stagnation
at work (by analogy to burnout, caused by the
stress of overwork).*

satiety
*The state of having had enough or too much of
something.*

Satiety is doubtless a key element in
boredom. Someone has written that the
only thing worse in life than not getting
any of what one has struggled for is to
get all of it.

ROBERT NISBET

self-torturing inertia

You're bored and depressed so you neglect what you're supposed to be doing, then feel guilty for not doing it, which bores and depresses you even more.

stir crazy

Prison slang for madness induced by the crushing boredom of incarceration.

stultify

To impair or invalidate through boredom or repetition.

London society has disintegrated. Those who should comprise it are scattered; most have retreated to their country houses. The rest are dispersed from central Africa to the West Indies. Those who should enliven it are stultifying and vulgarizing themselves before the television.

Evelyn Waugh (1959)

surfeit
A sickening or boring excess; the revulsion of overindulgence.

taedium vitae
"Weariness of life"; the ancient Roman version of ennui, mentioned by Aurus Gellius in the year 150.

terminal ennui
Severe boredom resulting in suicide.

vigilance decrement
Decline in work performance resulting from boredom, especially in such "sustained attention" jobs as airport security screener and production inspector.

visual motor ecstasy

Inability of young people to engage in long-term thinking, a phenomenon identified by University of North Carolina pediatrics professor Mel Levine whereby any cultural artifact that doesn't deliver instant gratification is considered boring by the "echo boomer" generation raised on video games, sound bites, and highlight reels:

I talked to the CEO of a major corporation recently and I said, "What characterizes your youngest employees nowadays?" . . . and he said, "There's one major thing. They can't think long-range. Everything has to be immediate, like a video game. And they have a lot of trouble sort of doing things in a stepwise fashion, delaying gratification. Really reflecting as they go along." I think that's new.

MEL LEVINE

weltschmerz

German for "world-pain," i.e., sadness over the vagaries of existence; spiritual exhaustion.

The world is sad, Oscar Wilde said, because a puppet was once melancholy. He was referring to Hamlet, a character he thought had taught the world a new kind of unhappiness—the unhappiness of eternal disappointment in life as it is, weltschmerz. Whether Shakespeare invented it or not, it has proved to be one of the most addictive of literary emotions. Readers consume volumes of it, and then ask to meet the author. It has also proved to be one of the most enduring of literary emotions, since life manages to come up short pretty reliably. Each generation feels disappointed in its own way, though, and seems to require its own literature of disaffection.

Louis Menand

l'atrophie de désir
Boredom during sex, a condition that, according to one survey, affects 23 percent of Frenchmen and 31 percent of Frenchwomen.

banal
Trite; commonplace; predictable.

blasé
Disinterested; the nonchalance of the hypersophisticated and overindulged.

boulevardier
An idler who hangs out in the cafés and bistros along the boulevards; a lounger.

cafard de grand luxe
Ennui induced by first-class travel.

ennui

Intense boredom; a condition of mental weariness resulting from lack of interest; listlessness and discontent brought on by the belief that life is essentially meaningless.

ennuyé

Bored, tired, weary; in a state of malaise; also, one so afflicted.

jejune

Dull, uninteresting; lacking in substance; empty.

longueur

A tedious passage in a work of music or literature.

malaise

A nonspecific, often lethargic sense of discontent.

métro-boulot-dodo

Slang roughly equivalent to "same old, same old," i.e., "subway, work, sleep," the daily grind of Parisian workers. From the poem "Couleurs d'usine" by Pierre Béarn: Métro boulot bistrots mégots dodo zero *("Subway work bars cigs sleep nothing").*

un moi avide du non-moi

Charles Baudelaire's phrase: "A self avid for non-self."

toujours perdrix

"Always partridge," i.e., too much of a good thing.

ver solitaire

The "solitary worm" of ennui that gnaws at the spirit, according to world-class ennuyé Madame du Deffand (see page 172).

CEDE THE DAY

The main thing is to never, ever work.
I just sit around all day doing what
Americans call hanging out. . . . I sit in
a room all day. I answer the phone. I do
crossword puzzles. I write letters. I open
a tin of soup or fry an egg. I wash my
socks. I file my nails. I do all the things
that other people do on their day off.
Except I do them every day.

QUENTIN CRISP

To do nothing at all is the most difficult
thing in the world, the most difficult and
the most intellectual.

OSCAR WILDE

I know perfectly well that I don't want
to do anything; to do something is to
create existence and there's quite enough
existence as there is.

JEAN-PAUL SARTRE

In America there is so much pressure about *work, work, work*, that it gets into your bones without your realizing it. It is a most unhealthy atmosphere. Work is very bad for you if too frequently engaged in.

GEORGE SANDERS

Work is a refuge of people who have nothing better to do.

OSCAR WILDE

My . . . desire as a boy was to retire. That ambition has never changed.

GEORGE SANDERS

Now, blessings light on him that first invented sleep! It covers a man all over, thoughts and all, like a cloak; it is meat for the hungry, drink for the thirsty, heat for the cold, and cold for the hot. It is the current coin that purchases all the pleasures of the world cheap, and

the balance that sets the king and the
shepherd, the fool and the wise man,
even.

MIGUEL DE CERVANTES

I have never taken any exercise except
sleeping and resting.

MARK TWAIN

He who sleeps half a day has won half
a life.

KARL KRAUS

In the summer I drink Guinness,
which requires no refrigeration and
no cooking—Guinness is a great day
shortener. If you get out of bed first
thing and drink a glass, then the day
doesn't begin until about twelve-thirty,
when you come to again, which is nice.
I try to live in a perpetual snooze.

QUENTIN CRISP

There is more refreshment and stimulation in a nap, even the briefest, than in all the alcohol ever distilled.

EDWARD LUCAS

Life is something to do when you can't get to sleep.

FRAN LEBOWITZ

Ever wake up in the middle of a really great dream to find you're back in your stinkin' life?

NORM MACDONALD

INDUCERS

AEROBICS

The word "aerobics" comes from two Greek words: *aero*, meaning "ability to," and *bics*, meaning "withstand tremendous boredom."

Dave Barry

THE AFTERLIFE

I don't believe in an afterlife, so I don't have to spend my whole life fearing hell, or fearing heaven even more. For whatever the tortures of hell, I think the boredom of heaven would be even worse.

Isaac Asimov

In heaven they will bore you, in hell you will bore them.

Katharine Whitehorn

AGING

Number one on my lengthening list
of the disadvantages of growing old is
the loss of my ability to be surprised.
Especially in the matter of humor. Sad to
say, it's been years since I fell out of my
chair laughing; I can't remember the last
aisle I rolled in. Today's comedy mostly
cheers me down. I have dumped so many
supposedly funny e-mailed jokes I have
developed a severe case of Delete Elbow.

LARRY GELBART

Boredom is the worst feeling there
is. Unfortunately, you don't sleep well,
or much, when you're seventy, and
afterward the day is long. I get up at
dawn, wash up, give myself a nice, close
shave, pick out a clean shirt, and that's it.
I don't have anything else to do. So out
I go, the way somebody would dive into
the endless sea from a boat that is slowly

sinking, and I head off in any direction, pounding my feet on the asphalt just to get away from the house, and from the thought of me, an old widower, sitting in an armchair.

Marco Lidoli

Discussing how old you are is the temple of boredom.

Ruth Gordon

AMUSEMENT

Amusements which do not amuse are among the most depressing of earthly evils. . . . We crave diversion so eagerly, we need it so sorely, that our disappointment in its elusiveness is fed by the flickerings of perpetual hope. Ennui has been defined as the desire for activity without the capacity for action, as a state of inertia quickened by discontent.

But it is rather a desire for amusement than for activity; it is a rational instinct warped by the irony of circumstances, and by our own selfish limitations.

AGNES REPPLIER

CAUTION

Monotony is the awful reward of the careful.

A. G. BUCKHAM

CHILDHOOD

Children are not oracles, but they ask with persistent regularity the great existential question, "What shall we do now?" Every adult remembers, among many other things, the great ennui of childhood, and every child's life is punctuated by spells of boredom: that state of suspended anticipation in which things are started and nothing begins, the mood of diffuse restlessness which contains that most absurd and paradoxical wish, the wish for a desire.

ADAM PHILLIPS

COMFORT

"Want and ennui," says Schopenhauer, "are the two poles of human life." The further we escape from one evil, the nearer we inevitably draw to the other. As soon as the first rude pressure of necessity is relieved, and man has leisure to think of something beyond his unsatisfied craving for food and shelter, then ennui steps in and claims him for her own. It is the price he pays, not merely for luxury, but for comfort.

AGNES REPPLIER

THE COUNTRY

I was happy when tea came. Such, I take it, is the state of those who live in the country. Meals are wished for from the cravings of vacuity of mind, as well as from the desire of eating. I was hurt to find even such a temporary feebleness, and that I was so far from being that robust wise man who is sufficient for his own happiness.

JAMES BOSWELL

The country has charms only for those not obliged to stay there.

ÉDOUARD MANET

DRY CLEANING

The Sisyphean cycle of dry cleaning: Waiting for your soiled garments to reach critical mass so you can take them to the dry cleaners; getting to the dry cleaners; waiting in line at the dry cleaners, wondering if the steamy chemical fumes are giving the employees tumors; giving the counter man your telephone number so he can "pull you up" on the computer; watching the counter man separate the pants and shirts; waiting for your receipt; getting home from the dry cleaners; waiting for your due date; getting to the dry cleaners to retrieve your dry cleaning; waiting in line while inhaling steamy chemical fumes, wondering . . . etc.; giving the counter man your telephone number, etc.; watching the conveyor trundle around, hoping your garments are actually on it; swiping your credit card and hoping it will go through; lifting your stack of dry cleaning off the hook; getting your dry cleaning home; putting your dry cleaning back in the closet, removing the plastic bags and cardboard packaging, pulling the tabs out of the

button holes in your shirts, unstuffing
the tissue paper from the sleeves of your
jackets, wondering how you're going
to dispose of the hangers, all the while
feeling guilty about the waste; inhaling
the chemical fumes in your closet,
wondering if they're giving *you* a tumor;
waiting for your soiled garments to
reach critical mass so you can take them
to the dry cleaners; getting to the dry
cleaners. . . .

HOWARD OGDEN

EDUCATION

I was thought to be reasonably intelligent
by the various schools I attended;
certainly, I was often more widely—if
eccentrically—read than many of my
teachers, which was not saying much;
unfortunately for me—and irritatingly
for them—I have never been so bored,
before or since, as I was by the courses
that I was obliged to take and pass. For

an energetic mind, with a passion to know everything, to be confined to translating from the Latin that dismal miniaturist Cornelius Nepo was exquisite torture, particularly when I was being denied, at least in class, Suetonius, Juvenal, Tacitus—and Livy, whom I had read at seven, in English. Worse, what passed for education in those days involved the memorizing of everything from Latin subjunctive verbs to mathematical theorems. Outside reading was not encouraged; neither was thought.

GORE VIDAL

School for most young people is a dull and uninspiring place to be in. Far from nurturing youngsters into expressive, intellectually alive and curious, confident, and able beings, school for many American youths is a trial to be endured. Boredom is so common that many consider it a normal phase of growing up.

MIHALY CSIKSZENTMIHALYI
AND JEREMY P. HUNTER

What is the task of all higher education?
  To make a machine of man.

What are the means to this end?
  The student must learn to be bored.

FRIEDRICH WILHELM NIETZSCHE

It is tiresome to hear education discussed, tiresome to educate, and tiresome to be educated.

LORD MELBOURNE

Thiebauld tells us that a prize-essay on
Ennui was read to the Academy of Berlin,
which put all the judges to sleep.

MARIA EDGEWORTH

ENTERTAINMENT

Despite its extraordinary variety of
diversions and resources, its frenzy for
spectacles and its feverish pursuit of
entertainment, America is bored. The
abundance of efforts made in the United
States to counter boredom have defeated
themselves, and boredom has become
the disease of our time.

JUDSON GOODING

The same machinery of modernism that
mass-produced . . . everyday conditions
of boredom has been credited with
mass-producing their counterweight
and corrective: a new cultural world

of mediated entertainments and pre-arranged excitements, available to the production clerk and the professor alike. And yet, it seems, each assembled moment of excitement has served only to amplify the rhythmic vacancy of everyday life.

JEFF FERRELL

FAMILY

Family dinners are more often than not an ordeal of nervous indigestion, preceded by hidden resentment and ennui and accompanied by psychosomatic jitters.

M. F. K. FISHER

Kingsley's preference for reading over "family conversation" was another source of trouble with father, and sometimes with mother as well. Anything suggesting the value of intellectual privacy, if not secrecy, struck them as slightly sinister. It was made clear to this already intense young scholar that "reading in public was deemed rude, while reading in private was deemed anti-social." What was demanded was the loathed experience of "joining in the family circle." Kingsley also disappointed father by his want of skill in cricket, a game father played with distinction. In sum, boredom, Amis asserts, was his main response to his father's presence, and the boredom increased with his aging parent's bent towards irrelevant anecdotal narrative late in life. The mature Amis now recognizes that his father must have been equally bored by his accounts of university and army life and the like, and he is led, now, to this conclusion: "It is depressing to think how persistently dull and egotistical we can be to those we most value, and how restless and peevish we get when they do it back to us." But it's hard to do much about this terrible fact, he observes, "given the burning sincerity of all boredom."

PAUL FUSSELL

FASCINATION

Boredom is just the reverse side of fascination: both depend on being outside rather than inside a situation, and one leads to the other.

SUSAN SONTAG

FLYING

Flying is hours and hours of boredom sprinkled with a few seconds of sheer terror.

GREGORY "PAPPY" BOYINGTON

GOD

The chief contribution of Protestantism to human thought is its massive proof that God is a bore.

H. L. MENCKEN

GRADUATIONS

Sometimes when I can't sleep, instead of counting sheep I count graduation speakers. As soon as I imagine the opening strains of Sir Edward Elgar's stately "Pomp and Circumstance," a great somnolence settles over me. Dum, dum da dum, dum dum. In my mind I am sitting on a folding chair under a sleepy sun. Instead of white sheep jumping over a fence, I see black academic robes swaying slowly in monotonous procession down an endless aisle. A speaker is introduced, and he steps to the lectern holding a thick sheaf of paper. He thanks a dozen people. Then he tells a joke and begins his speech. Time passes. The valedictorian hasn't even started yet. More time passes. The speaker is on his third point. An idle bee bumps against the edge of the stage. The speaker drones on and on. . . .

Why are graduations so crushingly soporific? Perhaps it's because the change we celebrate—the transformation of student into adult—is a huge change, a change almost too great to comprehend. It makes us cry and it makes us cheer. It's all a bit too much, so we take refuge in what Wordsworth called "the balm that tames all anguish"—in other words, 40 winks. The ceremony promotes it, and we're grateful.

SUSAN CHEEVER

GREAT BOOKS

Have I uttered the fundamental blasphemy, that once said sets the spirit free? The literature of the past is a bore—when one has said that frankly to oneself, then one can proceed to qualify and make exceptions.

Oliver Wendell Holmes, Jr.

INCARCERATION

I think the deadening monotony, the bickering, the boredom are peculiar to the convalescent ward. I speak about it to Georgie Small—the old-timer who should know.

"Ennui!" he tells me. "Ennui and incarceration are synonymous. Our mentors, precariously balanced upon the diametrically opposed concepts of punishment and rehabilitation, are incapable of resolving the situation into a workable pattern. Punishment and rehabilitation! One negates the other and any action in one direction provokes violent reaction from the other. Result? Stalemate in all penological echelons. Nothing is done and we do nothing. Since we are individuals who perform primarily by action, a cessation of such action ineluctably stultifies, distorts, demeans, dehumanizes even the strongest of us."

Noodles, listening in, shakes his head in bewilderment. He explains it in his own way. "Buddy, all I know is in this goddam place the only thing ya kin do is blow ya top!"

JOHN RESKO

LEISURE

Boredom is the malaise of our civilization, with its relatively large amounts of leisure time, and . . . this sickness is manifested both in the wide spread of acute boredom and in the frantic activities to escape boredom.

ERNEST SCHACHTEL

The idea that leisure is of value in itself is only conditionally true. The average man simply spends his leisure as a dog spends it. His recreations are all puerile, and the time supposed to benefit him really only stupefies him.

H. L. MENCKEN

We aren't built for free time as a species. We think we are, but we aren't.

DOUGLAS COUPLAND

LIFE ITSELF

Life, friends, is boring. We must not say so.

JOHN BERRYMAN

Known under several aliases—anguish, ennui, tedium, the doldrums, humdrum, the blahs, apathy, listlessness, stolidity, lethargy, languor, etc.—boredom is a complex phenomenon and by and large a product of repetition. It would seem, then, that the best remedy against it would be constant inventiveness and originality. . . . Alas, life won't supply you with that option, for life's main medium is precisely repetition.

JOSEPH BRODSKY

Life . . . oscillates between these two terms: suffering, that opens a window on the real, and is the main condition of the artistic experience; and boredom, that must be considered as the most tolerable, because it is the most durable of human evils.

SAMUEL BECKETT

Living, just by itself—what a dirge that is! Life is a classroom and Boredom's the usher, there all the time to spy on you; whatever happens, you've got to look as if you were awfully busy all the time doing something that's terribly exciting—or he'll come along and nibble your brain.

LOUIS-FERDINAND CÉLINE

You live eighty years, and at best you get about six minutes of pure magic.

GEORGE CARLIN

Life, Lady Stutfield, is simply a *mauvais quart d'heure* made up of exquisite moments.

OSCAR WILDE

Estragon: Charming spot. Inspiring
    prospects. Let's go.
Clov: Do you believe in the life to come?
Hamm: Mine was always that.

SAMUEL BECKETT

And the days are not full enough
And the nights are not full enough,
And life slips by like a field-mouse
Not shaking the grass.

EZRA POUND

For I have known them all already,
    known them all—
Have known the evenings, mornings,
    afternoons,
I have measured out my life with coffee
    spoons.

T. S. ELIOT

I wore a neck brace for about a year. I wasn't injured, I just got tired of holding my head up.

MARGARET SMITH

LOVE

When you're away, I'm restless, lonely,
Wretched, bored, dejected; only
Here's the rub, my darling dear,
I feel the same when you are here.

SAMUEL HOFFENSTEIN

Tristan and Isolde were lucky to die when they did. They'd have been sick of all that rubbish in a year.

ROBERTSON DAVIES

Do you love me
Or do you not?
You told me once,
But I forgot.

ANONYMOUS (QUOTED BY DICK CAVETT)

LUXURY

Charlie ran the light on Santa Monica
and headed north past the eclectic
rows of Taj Mahals on either side of
the wide street. A 450 SL pulled up
beside them at a stop sign. A woman in
tennis whites was at the wheel, her hair
tied back fashionably, her long tanned
fingers absently drumming a rhythm on
the wheel. In her lap, an immaculately
groomed poodle sat contentedly. On
the woman's face was a trace of supreme
ennui, matched perfectly by the poodle.
The Ennui Sisters.

PETER LEFCOURT

I rather like bad wine . . . one gets so
bored with good wine.

BENJAMIN DISRAELI

What would life be without coffee? But
then, what is it even with coffee?

LOUIS XV

About ten days' extravagance is enough
before the *cafard de grand luxe* sets in and
there emerges the point of tension which
will become intolerable; the pianist in
the bar who projects his personality, the
electric clock that suppresses a click
before not striking, the staring lift-boy,
the concierge who seems to know too
much about us.

CYRIL CONNOLLY

MARRIAGE

Marriage is a kind of cosmic, bored familiarity in which everyone watches television, and lives and lets live.

MICHAEL NOVAK

I have known couples who, unable to tolerate the sight or sound of each other, devote all their energies to trapping guests. Their dinner tables are always filled with strange nervous people who have never seen each other before, having been run down and bagged on different heaths.

I have found myself often at such repasts, and have sat twitching for hours while husband and wife tried to turn me into entertainment. Little entertainment is possible in the arenas of boredom. The guests usually end with a distaste for each other similar to the aversion between the married couple hosting them. And they

leave on the single note of comradeli-
ness—that nothing can ever drag them to
that house again, where everybody felt at
his worst and performed at his lowest.

I have learned not to feel sorry for
such hosts and hostesses because I have
seen that their dinner parties are never
failures in their own eyes. A battle has
been won, not lost. The married pair
have managed to lessen their boredom by
grandly sharing it.

BEN HECHT

He married a woman to stop her getting
    away
Now she's there all day.

PHILIP LARKIN

THE MEDIA

It is the excruciating, unrelenting stream of electronic- and print-generated bilge that drives the boredom-intolerant person to full-blown acedia.

KATHERINE A. POWERS

You know how on the evening news they always tell you that the stock market is up in active trading, or off in moderate trading, or trading in mixed activity, or whatever? Well, who gives a shit?

DAVE BARRY

MODERN TECHNOLOGY

By his very success in inventing labor-saving devices, modern man has manufactured an abyss of boredom that only the privileged classes in earlier civilizations have ever fathomed.

LEWIS MUMFORD

Taking a shower, brushing one's teeth, eating a bowl of cereal [and] hundreds of other peaceful activities have been tarted up with flavorings and music and gadgetry, so that after a brief period of novelty they become not bland and comfortingly familiar but irritatingly boring.

Mary Catherine Bateson

A culture frantic to entertain, stimulate, divert and inform us is in no danger of drowning out boredom. If anything, it may make that placid sense of turning off and turning away, buoyantly detached and rising to the opportunity, more valuable than ever.

Steven Winn

MONOGAMY

The great thing about sex with whores
is the excitement and variety. If you say
you're enjoying sex with the same person
after a couple of years you're either a
liar or on something. Of all the sexual
perversions, monogamy is the most
unnatural. Most of our affairs run the
usual course. Fever. Boredom. Trapped.
This explains much of the friction in our
lives—love being the delusion that one
woman differs from another. But with
brothels there is always the exhilaration
of not knowing what you're going to get.

SEBASTIAN HORSLEY

NATURE

Nature . . . has had her day; she has
finally and utterly exhausted the patience
of sensitive observers by the revolting
uniformity of her landscapes and
skyscapes. After all, what platitudinous

limitations she imposes, like a tradesman
specializing in a single line of business;
what petty-minded restrictions, like
a shopkeeper stocking one article to
the exclusion of all others; what a
monotonous store of meadows and
trees, what a commonplace display of
mountains and seas!

J. K. HUYSMANS

What is there to make so much of in
the Thames? I am quite tired of it. Flow,
flow, flow, always the same.

MARQUESS OF QUEENSBURY

PARADISE

I've lived in good climate, and it bores
the hell out of me. I like weather rather
than climate.

JOHN STEINBECK

Oh don't the days seem lank and long
When all goes right and nothing goes
    wrong,
And isn't your life extremely flat
With nothing whatever to grumble at!

W. S. GILBERT

Oh God, not another fucking beautiful
day.

JAMES FOX

I never saw a people that seemed so
hopelessly bored as the Tahitians. [As for
the Samoans] I believe that ennui is the
chief cause of their wars.

HENRY ADAMS

PARENTS AND PARENTHOOD

If parents would only realize how they bore their children!

GEORGE BERNARD SHAW

A child of my own! Oh, no, no, no! Let my flesh perish with me, and let me not transmit to anyone the boredom and the ignominiousness of life.

GUSTAVE FLAUBERT

PEOPLE

People always get tired of one another. I grow tired of myself whenever I am left alone for ten minutes, and I am certain that I am fonder of myself than anyone can be of another person.

GEORGE BERNARD SHAW

My friends are all either married, boring, and depressed; single, bored, and depressed; or moved out of town to avoid boredom and depression.

Douglas Coupland

Chief among the activities that bore me—because I cannot give sufficient attention and my mind wanders and I want to be doing something else—is talking with other human beings. When my friend sits across the room from me I become impatient. I complained to A. about this reclusiveness, and he imagined a scene I had already thought of. As I am sitting in the living room talking to my friend Z., with whom I enjoy a correspondence, after twenty or thirty minutes I am bored and restless. I want to go off into my study, close the door, and be alone—where I would be perfectly happy to write a letter to Z.

Donald Hall

The world is full of people who are not worth speaking to.

Voltaire

I can sympathize with people's pains, but *not* with their pleasure. There is something curiously boring about somebody else's happiness.

Aldous Huxley

The trouble with dreams, of course, is that other people's are so boring.

W. H. Auden

The capacity of human beings to bore
one another seems to be vastly greater
than that of any other animals. Some of
their most esteemed inventions have no
other apparent purpose, for example, the
dinner party of more than two, the epic
poem, and the science of metaphysics.

H. L. MENCKEN

There are no uninteresting things, only
uninteresting people.

G. K. CHESTERTON

There is a certain weary look that
appears on the faces of those who are
bored. Look out for the weary look
when you associate with people.

E. W. HOWE

POETRY READINGS

It would be very odd to go to a concert hall and discover that the pianist on offer *wasn't any good at all*, in the sense that he couldn't actually play the piano. But in poetry this is an experience we've learnt to take in our stride.

JAMES FENTON

PORNOGRAPHY

I don't think pornography is very harmful, but it is terribly, terribly boring.

NOEL COWARD

My reaction to porno films is as follows: After the first ten minutes, I want to go home and screw. After the first twenty minutes, I never want to screw again as long a I live.

ERICA JONG

POVERTY

Boredom is the keynote of poverty . . .
for where there is no money there is no
change of any kind, not of scene or of
routine.

MOSS HART

As for poverty, boredom is the most
brutal part of its misery, and the
departure from it takes more radical
forms: of violent rebellion or drug
addiction. Both are temporary, for
the misery of poverty is infinite; both,
because of that infinity, are costly. In
general, a man shooting heroin into
his vein does so largely for the same
reason you buy a video: to dodge the
redundancy of time. The difference,
though, is that he spends more than he's
got, and that his means of escape become
as redundant as what he is escaping from
faster than yours. On the whole, the

difference in tactility between a syringe's needle and a stereo's push button roughly corresponds to that between the acuteness and dullness of time's impact upon the have-nots and the haves.

Joseph Brodsky

The poor get bored, the rich have ennui.

Howard Ogden

PRIVILEGE

Nothing is more striking throughout history than the chronic disaffection, the malaise, the anxiety, and the psychotic self-destructiveness of the ruling classes, once they are in command of "all that the heart can desire." For the dominant minority, the privileged few, have always been faced with the ultimate curse of such a meaningless existence: sheer boredom.

LEWIS MUMFORD

They were four married couples, and they had been boys and girls together, and they had a son and daughter apiece, and they all went to the same dentist. The one [Mrs. Richard Norton] had a small oval face, small breasts, blue eyes, thin arms, no expression, no blood: literally, of course, not genealogically. One of them stared with wide blue eyes right into people's faces, and blinked vaguely. She was lovely. These eight young people were very happy. They ignored everything but themselves, in whom they were not very interested. Presently, a Prince of the blood [the Prince of Wales] joined them, there was a little stir for a minute or two, a little laughter, and then he rose to dance with the girl of the bright blue eyes. As she danced she stared thoughtfully at the glass dome of the ceiling. She looked bored with boredom.

MICHAEL ARLEN

PUBLICITY

How dreary to be somebody!
How public, like a frog
To tell your name the livelong day
To an admiring bog!

EMILY DICKINSON

I'm rather bored by the subject—
meaning me. It's a sort of a yoke, but
at times you know, a yoke is a kind of
comfort. And it's always there.

LAURENCE OLIVIER

RELAXATION

There is nothing so insupportable to man as complete repose, without passion, occupation, amusement, care. Then it is that he feels his nothingness, his isolation, his insufficiency, his dependence, his impotence, his emptiness.

BLAISE PASCAL

ROUTINE

The safety of routines protects you from risk of failure. But it can also be a trap.

MIHALY CSIKSZENTMIHALYI

To do the same thing over and over is not only boredom; it is to be controlled by rather than to control what you do.

HERACLITUS

It is said of an Englishman that he hanged himself to avoid the daily task of dressing and undressing.

JOHANN WOLFGANG VON GOETHE

THE SABBATH

The social representation of boredom is Sunday.

ARTHUR SCHOPENHAUER

Millions long for immortality who do not know what to do with themselves on a rainy Sunday afternoon.

SUSAN ERTZ

SEX

Fucking's boring.

LARRY DAVID

SMALL TALK

I am bored with gabbers and their gab;
my soul abhors them. . . . Is there any
place where there is no traffic in empty
talk? Is there on this earth one who does
not worship himself talking?

KAHLIL GIBRAN

SMALL TOWNS

Oh, whatever happened to the past,
when I was young and happy and
intelligent, when I dreamed wonderful
dreams and thought great thoughts,
when my life and my future were shining
with hope? What happened to it? We
barely begin to live, when all of a sudden
we're old and boring and lazy and useless
and unhappy. This town has a hundred
thousand people in it, and not one of
them has ever amounted to a thing. Each
one is just like all the others: they eat,
drink, sleep, and then they die . . . more

of them are born, and they eat, drink, and sleep too, and then because they're bored they gossip, they drink, they gamble, they sue each other, the wives cheat on the husbands and the husbands lie, they pretend they don't see anything or hear anything, and the children end up just as aimless and dead as their parents.

ANTON CHEKHOV

SOPHISTICATION

The more refined one is, the more unhappy.

ANTON CHEKHOV

THE SOUTH

Southern white speech drawls with ennui, frustration, and repressed hostility. The tensions of life in the South make most Southern women nonstop chatterers.

ASHLEY MONTAGU

SPORTS

I was compelled to play games [at school]. I believe the ball, with the exception of the wheel, was the greatest single disaster of mankind.

ROBERT MORLEY

One reason I didn't like football was the boredom of putting on and taking off all that gear.

GORE VIDAL

I always thought it was boring.

RYAN JARONCYK

(N.Y. METS FIRST-ROUND DRAFT PICK, ON WHY
HE RETIRED FROM BASEBALL AT THE AGE OF 20)

THE SUBURBS

Slums may well be breeding-grounds
of crime, but middle-class suburbs are
incubators of apathy and delirium.

CYRIL CONNOLLY

SUCCESS

Unless one is taught what to do with
success after getting it, achievement
of it must inevitably leave him prey to
boredom.

BERTRAND RUSSELL

Now and then you describe to yourself what it's like on paper, and shouldn't you feel better? It's very hard to experience things. There's a very specific feeling when it's 10:30 and you're back at the hotel with your Oscar and your club sandwich, and you can't call anybody, because they all think you're at the Governor's Ball.

MIKE NICHOLS

The penalty for success is to be bored by the people who used to snub you.

NANCY ASTOR

TELEVISION

The television, that insidious beast, that Medusa which freezes a billion people to stone every night, staring fixedly, that Siren which called and sang and promised so much and gave, after all, so little.

RAY BRADBURY

I visited a friend who'd just got satellite TV—two hundred digital-quality channels. He ushered me into the "media room" (i.e., den), handed me a drink, and sat me down on the sofa in front of a 42-inch plasma screen, which was . . . off.

"Why isn't the television on?" I asked.

"Oh, there's nothing on *now*," he said.

HOWARD OGDEN

TIME

When we are bored, our attitude toward time is altered, as it is in some dreamlike states. Time seems endless, there is no distinction between past, present, and future. There seems to be only an endless present.

MARTIN WAUGH

The concept of boredom entails an inability to use up present moments in a personally fulfilling way.

WAYNE DYER

To fill the hour—that is happiness.

RALPH WALDO EMERSON

TIPS FOR BEATING BOREDOM

Why is it that no other species but man gets bored? Under the circumstances in which a man gets bored, a dog goes to sleep. Thought Experiment: Imagine that you are a member of a tour visiting Greece. The group goes to the Parthenon. It is a bore. Few people even bother to look—it looked better in the brochure. So people take half a look, mostly take pictures, remark on the serious erosion by acid rain. You are puzzled. Why should one of the glories and fonts of Western civilization, viewed under pleasant conditions—good weather, good hotel room, good food, good guide—be a bore? Now imagine under what set of circumstances a viewing of the Parthenon would not be a bore. For example, you are a NATO colonel defending Greece against a Soviet assault. You are in a bunker in downtown Athens, binoculars propped on sandbags. It is dawn. A medium-range missile attack is under way. Half a million Greeks are dead. Two missiles bracket the Parthenon. The next will surely be a hit. Between columns of smoke, a ray of golden light catches the portico. Are you bored? Can you see the Parthenon?

WALKER PERCY

In New York City, my hometown, the way to make a bus come is to light a cigarette. Not a puff later, the transit arrives. Now that we've all quit smoking, we don't make buses materialize anymore and must learn patience and other coping techniques. To dispel the angst of waiting, subtle exercises are best, the kind that won't have fellow travelers quietly distancing themselves from you: cannonball rolls for your neck, shrugs for your shoulders, carpal tunnel exercises for your wrists and fingers. Keep a sonnet in your wallet and memorize it. The best technique is speaking to a stranger or asking a child about her favorite video game.

AIDA PAVLETICH

TRAVEL

I was glad to go abroad, and, perhaps, glad to come home, which is, in other words, I was, I am afraid, weary of being at home, and weary of being abroad. Is not this the state of life?

SAMUEL JOHNSON

Pack the one bag. Unpack it, pack it, unpack it, pack it: passport, ticket, book, taxi, airport, check-in, beer, announcement, stairs, airplane, fasten seat-belt, airborne, flight, rocking, sun, stars, space, hips of strolling stewardesses, read, sleep, clouds, falling engine speed, descent, circling, touch

down, earth, unfasten seat-belt, stairs,
airport, immunization book, visa,
customs, questions, taxi, streets, houses,
people, hotel, key, room, stuffiness,
thirst, otherness, foreignness, loneliness,
fatigue, life.

RYSZARD KAPUSCINSKI

Moments of travel ennui or traveler's
panic we have all felt: The sheer inability
to eat another wonton, the desperate
wish to be transported by instantaneous
space/time travel into one's own bed.

DIANE JOHNSON

I am now in a beautiful town in Tuscany.
I am well thought of by all the nobility.
I enjoy the honest friendship of some
pleasant ladies. I am studying the
beautiful Italian language and making

good progress. I am also studying music with an excellent teacher; I play my flute and sing with real enjoyment. I am enjoying good health. The weather is clear and agreeable. I can do everything I wish. I am in a situation which I imagined in my most delicious moments. And yet I cannot say I am happy. I am surprised at this. I don't know what to think. I don't know what to look for. Undoubtedly, in this world no man can be completely happy.

JAMES BOSWELL

Travel is the most private of pleasures. There is no greater bore than the travel bore. We do not in the least want to hear what he has seen in Hong Kong.

VITA SACKVILLE-WEST

VIRTUE

I think mankind by thee would be less
  bored
If only thou wert not thine own reward.

JOHN KENDRICK BANGS

Virtuous people often revenge themselves
for the constraints to which they submit
by the boredom which they inspire.

GUSTAVE LE BON

Morality is a venereal disease. Its
primary stage is called virtue; its
secondary stage, boredom; its tertiary
stage, syphilis.

KARL KRAUS

WAITING

I read somewhere that we spend a full third of our lives waiting. I've also read that we spend a third of our lives sleeping, a third working, and a third at our leisure. Now either somebody's lying, or we're spending all our leisure time waiting to go to work or sleep.

TOM BODETT

Estragon: I'm tired! (*Pause.*) Let's go.
Vladimir: We can't.
Estragon: Why not?
Vladimir: We're waiting for Godot.
Estragon: Ah! (*Pause. Despairing.*)
   What'll we do, what'll we do!
Vladimir: There's nothing we can do.

SAMUEL BECKETT

WHINING

The world is quickly bored by the recital of misfortune and willingly avoids the sight of distress.

W. Somerset Maugham

WORK

Just after 2:00 A.M., Dag got off shift at Larry's Bar where, along with me, he is a bartender. While the two of us were walking home, he ditched me right in the middle of a conversation we were having and darted across the road, where he then scraped a boulder across the front hood and windshield of a Cutlass Supreme. This is not the first time he has vandalized like this. The car was the color of butter and bore a bumper sticker saying WE'RE SPENDING OUR CHILDREN'S INHERITANCE, a message that I suppose irked Dag, who was bored and cranky after eight hours of working his McJob ("Low pay, low prestige, low benefits, low future").

DOUGLAS COUPLAND

If you were searching for a word to describe the conversations that go on down the mine, boring would spring to your lips. Oh, God! They're very boring. If you ever want to hear things like: "Hello, I've found a bit of coal." "Have you really?" "Yes, no doubt about it, this black substance is coal all right." "Jolly good, the very thing we're looking for." It's not enough to keep the mind alive, is it?

PETER COOK

WORLD WAR II

If you were a civilian, daily life was boring. If you were a soldier, daily life was very boring. But it was most boring to be a prisoner of war. By establishing the principle that captured officers were to do no work and that NCOs could work only as supervisors of the work of privates, the Geneva Convention guaranteed that life in POW camps would be for many an experience of unprecedented ennui, against which some often fantastic defenses were required. In one German *stalag*, an American lieutenant with nothing to do "counted the barbs in one section of the barbed wire fence and then estimated the total number of barbs around the encampment. When he announced this number, his fellow kriegies not only didn't consider him mad, they formed teams to check him out with a barb-by-barb count." There certainly was

little escape from boredom to be had
by moving upwards, toward high ranks
and the centers of power. One of the
most tedious places during the whole
war was Hitler's own dinner table,
which he dominated with interminable
nightly monologues on strategy,
history, eugenics, and what have you.
Even his toads found the boredom of
this unvarying *Tishgespräche* almost
unendurable. Generals and field marshals
nodded, and Albert Speer recalls "the
sense of stifling boredom."

PAUL FUSSELL

PALLIATIVES

This is the curse of our age, even the strangest aberrations are no cure for boredom.

STENDHAL

ADRENALIN

Adrenalin dispels boredom. Run, you sufferers from ennui! Run for your lives!

MASON COOLEY

Bungee-jumping . . . in which you throw yourself from a bridge into a ravine with a long piece of knicker elastic tied between your belt and the bridge—had originated in New Zealand. Only in a culture of unusual monotony could such a practice have become established. It resulted, presumably, from the desperate need for a buzz. Bungee-jumping would never have begun in New York, where you could get much the same adrenalin rush just by going out to buy a loaf of bread.

MARK LAWSON

They sicken of the calm, who knew the storm.

DOROTHY PARKER

ARSON

Boredom Incited 2 Firefighters Charged in Arson, Marshal Says

Two Marbury volunteer firefighters were charged last week with arson in connection with an August 2000 fire set at an unoccupied camper trailer on Bicknell Road, according to the State Fire Marshal's Office. . . .

Authorities said [the men] set the fire
because they were bored and wanted to
respond to a fire.

Washington Post

ASSAULT WITH
A DEADLY WEAPON

I had a boring day.

Jeffrey Farina

(explaining why he shot one person
and stabbed three others in a fast-food
restaurant; *U.S. News & World Report*)

AUTOMOBILES

I tend to buy cars for the fun of it. I drive
them around for three weeks and then I
get bored, dump them in the garage and
let the batteries go completely flat.

Eddie Murphy

When I get real bored, I like to drive downtown and get a great parking spot, then sit in my car and count how many people ask me if I'm leaving.

STEVEN WRIGHT

BOOKS

The one way of tolerating existence is to lose oneself in literature, as in a perpetual orgy. . . . (The minute I no longer have a book on hand or am not dreaming of writing one, I could *howl* with boredom.)

GUSTAVE FLAUBERT

How are we to spend our lives, anyway? That is the real question. We read to seek the answer, and the search itself—the task of a lifetime—becomes the answer.

LYNNE SHARON SCHWARTZ

CHARACTER

Some people, whether teenagers
or senior citizens, manage to find
constructive alternatives to boredom;
others don't. If I expect all my
stimulation to come from the outside,
then I would have a very low threshold
for boredom because I'm always going
to be waiting for things to appear to me,
[but] if I'm an individual who believes
my behavior and my emotions are
largely under my own control, I'm more
likely to find some internally generated
stimulation and I'll be less vulnerable to
boredom.

DANIEL TRESSLER

In order to live free and happily you must
sacrifice boredom. It is not always an
easy sacrifice.

RICHARD BACH

Never chain your dogs together with sausages. One must accustom one's self to be bored.

LADY BLOOMFIELD

CRUELTY

Idle people are often bored and bored people, unless they sleep a lot, are cruel. It is no accident that boredom and cruelty are great preoccupations in our time.

RENATA ADLER

Wars, pogroms, and persecution have all been part of the flight from boredom. . . . Boredom is therefore a vital problem for the moralist, since at least half the sins of mankind are caused by the fear of it.

BERTRAND RUSSELL

CURIOSITY

The cure for boredom is curiosity. There is no cure for curiosity.

ELLEN PARR

DELINQUENCY

Having spent some months in the streets with boys of an American gang, I came away with certain impressions, all of which stemmed from a single, overwhelming conviction—that the problem underneath is boredom. And it is not strange, after all, that this should be so. It is the theme of so many of our novels, our plays, and especially our movies in the past twenty years and is the hallmark of society as a whole. The outcry of Britain's so-called Angry Young Men was against precisely this seemingly universal sense of life's pointlessness, the absence of any apparent aim to it all. So many

American books and articles attest to the same awareness here. The stereotype of the man coming home from work and staring dumbly at a television set is an expression of it, and the "New Wave" of movies in France and Italy propound the same fundamental theme. People no longer seem to know why they are alive; existence is simply a string of near experiences marked off by periods of stupefying spiritual and psychological stasis, and the good life is basically an amused one.

ARTHUR MILLER (1962)

DISENGAGEMENT

What's wrong with dropping out? To me, this is the whole point: one's right to withdraw from a social environment that offers no spiritual sustenance, and to *mind one's business.*

WILLIAM S. BURROUGHS

ENGAGEMENT

We act as though comfort and luxury
were the chief requirements of life, when
all that we need to make us happy is
something to be enthusiastic about.

ALBERT EINSTEIN

I have to have something to do that
engages me totally. Without that, life
is hell for me. I can't be idle and I don't
know what to do other than write. If
I were afflicted with some illness that
left me otherwise OK but stopped me
writing, I'd go out of my mind. I don't
really have other interests. My interest
is in solving the problems presented by
writing a book. That's what stops my
brain spinning like a car wheel in the
snow, obsessing about nothing. Some
people do crossword puzzles to satisfy

their need to keep the mind engaged. For me, the absolutely demanding mental test is the desire to get the work right.

PHILIP ROTH

The moment we indulge our affections, the earth is metamorphosed, there is no winter and no night; all tragedies, all ennuis, vanish, all duties even.

RALPH WALDO EMERSON

It is the unknown that excites the ardor of scholars, who, in the known alone, would shrivel up with boredom.

WALLACE STEVENS

FEAR

Fear is the best antidote for ennui. The early settlers of America, surrounded by hostile Indians, and doubtful each morning whether the coming nightfall would not see their rude homes given to the flames, probably suffered but little from the dullness which seems so oppressive to the peaceful agriculturist of today. The mediaeval women, who were content to pass their time in weaving endless tapestries, had less chance to complain of the monotony of life than their artistic, scientific, literary, and philanthropic sisters of our age; for at any hour, breaking in upon their tranquil labors, might be heard the trumpet's blast; at any hour might come the tidings, good or bad, which meant a few more years of security, or the horrors of siege and pillage.

AGNES REPPLIER

FASTING

A sure cure for boredom: fast until you are ravenous.

MASON COOLEY

FOOD

The one way to get thin is to reestablish a purpose in life. . . . Obesity is a mental state, a disease brought on by boredom and disappointment.

CYRIL CONNOLLY

No question looms larger on a daily basis for many of us than "What's for lunch?" and, when that has been resolved, "What's for dinner?" There have been mutterings that the whole food thing has gone too far in America, but I think not. Good food is a benign weapon against the sodden way we live.

JIM HARRISON

GAMBLING

Gaming relieved me from that insuperable listlessness by which I was oppressed. I became interested—I became agitated; in short, I found a new kind of stimulus, and I indulged in it most intemperately. I grew immoderately fond of that which supplied me with sensations. My days and nights were passed at the gaming-table.

MARIA EDGEWORTH

The next best thing to playing and winning is playing and losing. The main thing is to play.

NICK "THE GREEK" DANDALOS

GAMES

A stereotyped but unconscious despair is
concealed even under what are called the
games and amusements of mankind.

HENRY DAVID THOREAU

Man is so unhappy that he would
be bored even if he had no cause for
boredom, by the very nature of his
temperament, and he is so vain that,
though he has a thousand and one basic
reasons for being bored, the slightest
thing, like pushing a ball with a billiard
cue, will be enough to divert him.

BLAISE PASCAL

GOSSIP

Here, indeed, is the very soul and
essence of ennui; not the virtuous
sentiment which revolts at the disclosure

of another's faults, but that deep and deadly ennui of life which welcomes evil as a distraction. The same selfish lassitude which made the gladiatorial combats a pleasant sight for the jaded eyes which witnessed them finds relief for its tediousness today in the swift destruction of confidence and reputation.

AGNES REPPLIER

IMAGINATION

I have been aware of a boredom, a restlessness, that no ordinary friendship can satisfy; only an extraordinary one. I have grown tired of my lot, I suppose, and have wanted strenuously to change it. So I write, and I take a lot of long walks, and I ferment my ideas, and if I am lucky they come out as vivid as I should like real life to be.

ANITA BROOKNER

We are rightfully fearful of boredom and its negative consequences. Too much time and money, little purpose, and boredom are a lethal combination. In an attempt to save our children, we sign them up for sports and classes. We let them watch a crazy amount of television and spend days at the computer.

I want to allow my children to be bored while they are young and under my watchful eye. To measure it into their bones and muscles like a rare fuel to propel them forward. To preempt the time spent on television and organized activities and have them spend it instead on claiming their imaginations. For in the end, that is all we have. If a thing cannot be imagined first—a cake, a relationship, a cure for AIDS—it cannot be.

Life is bound by what we can envision. I cannot plant imagination into my children. I can, however, provide an environment where their creativity is not just another mess to clean up but welcome evidence of grappling successfully with boredom. It is possible for boredom to deliver us to our best selves, the ones that long for risk and illumination and unspeakable beauty. If we sit still long enough, we may hear the call behind boredom. With practice, we may have the imagination to rise up from the emptiness and answer.

NANCY H. BLAKEY

INTOXICATION

When you're drunk you're never bored. . . . The moments slip by in such a satisfactory way.

MICHAEL DOBBS

LOVE

To fall in love with a woman is to fall in love with life and with oneself. It is to overflow with hope and dread, to discover the only solution for ennui.

BEN HECHT

MENDACITY

Without lies humanity would perish of despair and boredom.

ANATOLE FRANCE

MINDFULNESS

Boredom can be an ally, a tool, and certainly a barometer of one's condition. When boredom arrives, notice what form it comes in, what exactly are the physical, mental, emotional and other subtle feelings or forms that you are labeling as boredom. Simply be aware of what arises and is imputed/assumed as boredom. But don't try to do anything about it—notice that "it too shall pass" into some other state. It is the noticing, the awareness of it, and the non-violent stance of simply being with it, not trying to change it or transform it, that is often the most direct and powerful way of transforming it.

PHIL SERVEDIO

NOVELTY

One factor, above all, helped to stave off boredom: the never-ending pursuit of novelty. "What do you have that's new and beautiful today?" Grace Wilson Vanderbilt would enquire of the clerks at Tiffany's on Fifth Avenue. Some took advance precautions against the malaise: At his villa at Californie on the heights above Cannes, the Russian

Prince Cherkassy employed 48 gardeners to change the flower beds overnight and thus surprise him each dawn.

RICHARD COLLIER

PSYCHIATRY

One should only see a psychiatrist out of boredom.

MURIEL SPARK

RESIGNATION

Good Lord, I don't know what "rights" a man has! And I don't know the solution of boredom. If I did, I'd be the one philosopher that had the cure for living. But I do know that about ten times as many people find their lives dull, and unnecessarily dull, as ever admit it; and I do believe that if we busted out and admitted it sometimes, instead of being nice and patient and loyal for sixty years,

and then nice and patient and dead for
the rest of eternity, why, maybe, possibly,
we might make life more fun.

SINCLAIR LEWIS

When hit by boredom, let yourself be
crushed by it; submerge, hit bottom. In
general, with things unpleasant, the
rule is: The sooner you hit bottom, the
faster you surface. The idea here is to
exact a full look at the worst. The reason
boredom deserves such scrutiny is that
it represents pure, undiluted time in all
its repetitive, redundant, monotonous
splendor.

JOSEPH BRODSKY

REST

Rest is a good thing, but boredom is its
brother.

VOLTAIRE

RISK

Risk is what separates the good part of life from the tedium.

JIMMY ZERO

RITUAL

The principal function of ritual in primitive society, it has been suggested by anthropologists, is to prevent boredom. Ritual punctuates the long and dreary sameness of life. . . . Through history and among all peoples religion generally has been a major antidote to what would otherwise be the sense of world-weariness, of passive indifference to life, in a great many minds. The religious "awakenings" which fill the history of religion in the West since the late Middle Ages have their roots, in some degree at least, in the desire for ecstatic release from tedium.

ROBERT NISBET

SELF-ABSORPTION

We feel safe, huddled within human institutions—churches, banks, madrigal groups—but these concoctions melt away at the basic moment. The self's responsibility, then, is to achieve rapport if not rapture with the giant, cosmic other: to appreciate, let's say, the walk back from the mailbox.

JOHN UPDIKE

If we were not all so interested in ourselves, life would be so uninteresting that none of us would be able to endure it.

ARTHUR SCHOPENHAUER

SEX

There comes a moment in the day,
when you have written your pages
in the morning, attended to your
correspondence in the afternoon, and
have nothing further to do. Then comes
that hour when you are bored; that's the
time for sex.

H. G. WELLS

UNCERTAINTY

Uncertainty and mystery are energies
of life. Don't let them scare you unduly,
for they keep boredom at bay and spark
creativity.

R. I. FITZHENRY

VANDALISM

I get bored, you see. When I get bored,
I rebel. I took me 'atchet and chopped
the 'otel room to bits. The lot of it. It
happens all the time.

KEITH MOON

WAR

Something must happen—and that
explains most human commitments . . .
even war.

ALBERT CAMUS

WORK

Anyone can do any amount of work . . .
provided it isn't the work he's supposed
to be doing at that moment.

ROBERT BENCHLEY

When I'm unhappy, I can't work. When I'm happy, I don't need to work. But when I don't need to work, I'm unhappy.

KENNETH TYNAN

Read. Do not brood. Immerse yourself in long study: only the habit of persistent work can make one continually content; it produces an opium that numbs the soul. I have lived through periods of atrocious ennui, spinning in a void, bored to distraction. One preserves oneself by dint of steadiness and pride. Try it.

GUSTAVE FLAUBERT

The life of the creative man is led, directed and controlled by boredom. Avoiding boredom is one of our most important purposes. It is also one of the most difficult . . . in the end, working is good because it is the last refuge of the man who wants to be amused.

SAUL STEINBERG

It seems to me that a great deal of nonsense is talked about the dignity of work. Work is a drug that dull people take to avoid the pangs of unmitigated boredom.

W. SOMERSET MAUGHAM

LAS SURFISTAS

BRAZIL—For the average American, North or South, the idea of ducking low overpasses, dodging 3,300-volt electrical wires, and maintaining one's balance, all while atop a subway train moving over fifty miles per hour, offers little appeal. However, the average American lives in a world where the comforting feeling of safety and responsibility outweighs the thrill of danger. Not in his entire lifetime will the average man experience such intensity as felt in a normal day of those of braver character. The average American lives in fear, quivering behind the transparent shield of feeble rationalizations. The average American does not privilege the rare honor of being one of the Jinxed.

Isares Goncalves do Nascimento, better known as Indio, is not the average American. At the tender age of 13, he was already surfing the roofs of commuter trains bound for Rio de Janeiro. By the time he was 19 he had become a true surfista. While pinguentes, or "hangers-on," cling to the side of the train below, surfistas stand on top, every muscle clenched to maintain the vital balance. Looking back on his first ride on the roof he says, "Once the train really started rolling, it was the most exciting thing I'd ever experienced. I was up there on top with my friends. The fresh air was smacking me in the face. It was the ultimate feeling of freedom. That's when I got hooked."

While admiring his courage, one must wonder whether the addictive thrill Indio describes is worth the risk. In 1989 alone gruesome train surfing accidents killed 150 Brazilian kids and injured 170 more. Others were horribly killed in the United States. Sixteen-year-old Roberto Rodriguez of Dobbs Ferry, New York, died on May 31, 1994, after having been knocked off the No. 2 train near the 149th St. station in the Bronx. On July 15, 1996, a young man died a similar death when he hit a signal light and was hurled onto the tracks while "subway surfing" the No. 2 train.

Attempts to stop train surfing have proved ineffective. Brazilian fines of 75 cents for the first attempt, 85 cents for the second are minuscule beside the awesome thrill of the surf, and, as New York Mayor Rudolph W. Guiliani points out, "There is no way you can protect a child who would choose to ride on top of a subway car." Indio's mother Juaquina would probably agree. Although completely aware of her son's habit, she has found no method of prevention. Feeling little hope, she says, "I can't believe my son is so stupid. Sooner or later, something will happen to him. It happens to all of them. They only stop surfing if they get badly injured—or if they die."

MARY DEYO, *Jinx Magazine*

LES ENNUYÉS
EXTRAORDINAIRES

Marie Antoinette (1755–1793)

Queen of France as the wife of Louis XVI, her extravagance and disdain for her subjects led to her execution by the Revolutionary Tribunal.

Marie Antoinette was especially infatuated with jewels. Many she bought on credit, and once, even though she had already exceeded her annual allowance by double, she purchased a pair of bracelets for 200,000 francs, then went to her husband, the king, to ask for a loan to help pay for it (he grudgingly helped her). Another time she swapped some of her diamonds to buy a pair of chandelier diamond earrings for 400,000 francs. When her own mother warned her about her buying habits, she told her not to worry, that it was just a "bagatelle."

She also helped popularize some of the extravagant styles of the day, such as a hairstyle in which the hair was piled at least a foot tall, sprinkled with a pound of powder and pomade, and topped with a coronet on which plumes of feathers, ribbons, flowers, and diamonds were further piled. Such a hairstyle did not stop her from pursuing one of her other interests—dancing—and she spent hours learning different dances and preparing for the balls. Her one guiding principle may have been her response to another caution from her mother about her actions. "I am so afraid of being bored," she explained.

M. HIRSH GOLDBERG

Michelangelo Antonioni (1912–)

*Acclaimed Italian director whose enigmatic, vaguely plotted films (*L'avventura, La notte*) depict the spiritual desolation of Europe after World War II. His characters seem to be looking for something, but don't know what it is, let alone where to find it. The critic David Thomson called him a "visionary* of emotional alienation," and termed his 1966 film, Blow-Up, a "beautiful inspection of emptiness."

It seems that boredom is one of the great discoveries of our time. If so, there's no question that he [Antonioni] must be considered a pioneer.

LUCHINO VISCONTI

Charles Baudelaire (1821–1867)

Self-proclaimed poète maudit *(accursed poet, i.e., one who is insufficiently appreciated), he filled his volume of poems,* The Flowers of Evil *(Les fleurs du mal; 1857), with "spleen and ennui."*

It is necessary to work, if not from inclination, at least from despair. Everything considered, work is less boring than amusing oneself.

I find the tedium of going to sleep and the tedium of waking up intolerable.

BAUDELAIRE'S SUICIDE NOTE

Alan Bennett (1934–)

British playwright, actor, and director perhaps best known as a member of the satirical revue Beyond the Fringe *(1960) and for* Talking Heads *(1988), a series of comic monologues.*

Shoveling coal [is] slightly less exhausting than traipsing around an art gallery.

The great advantage of being in a rut is that when one is in a rut, one knows exactly where one is.

Ingmar Bergman (1918–)

Swedish director whose haunting early films—The Seventh Seal *(1957),* Wild Strawberries *(1957),* The Virgin Spring *(1960)*—*gained him international fame.*

One of ennui's most terrible components is the overwhelming feeling of ennui that comes over you whenever you try to explain it.

Everything is worth precisely as much as a belch, the difference being that a belch is more satisfying.

Emma Bovary

Title character of Gustav Flaubert's Madame Bovary *(1857), a provincial housewife who seeks relief from ennui in romantic fantasies, adultery, and finally suicide.*

It is a generally accepted interpretation that Flaubert's Emma Bovary presents symptoms similar to those felt by the bored suburbanite. And yet to reduce her ennui to this level is to misunderstand the very complex condition of which she is a victim. The former suffers from a metaphysical malady, and the latter only feels a superficial and vague disquiet. It is this difference in dimension that makes of the one a great literary figure and of the other an undistinguished and uninteresting representative of a group.

REINHARD KUHN

E. M. Cioran (1911–1995)

Romanian novelist, essayist, and aphorist whose subjects are solitude, alienation, and boredom.

I . . . am very sensitive where boredom is concerned and I have been bored my whole life long. Everything in Russian literature revolves around boredom. It is the everyday nothingness. I have suffered through the phenomenon of boredom in an almost pathological way, I have been bored because I wanted to be bored. Indeed, if one is only bored, then everything is at an end. Boredom is connected naturally with time, with the horror of time, with the experience and the consciousness of time. Those who are not aware of time do not become

bored. Basically life is only possible
if one is not aware of time. If one
should happen to want to experience
consciously one of those moments that
pass, one would be lost; life would
become unbearable. The experience of
boredom is the result of the despair
of time.

Charlie Citrine

Narrator of Saul Bellow's Humboldt's Gift
*(1975), a successful novelist tortured by
boredom, which he defines as "a kind of pain
caused by unused powers, the pain of wasted
possibilities or talents." He sets out to write*
Great Bores of the Western World *on the
assumption that " from the beginning mankind
experienced states of boredom but that no one
had ever approached the matter front and
center as a subject in its own right."*

John Cleese (1939–)

British actor and comedian who became famous as a member of the Monty Python comedy group and went on to a successful career as an actor and commercial spokesman. He once told an interviewer: "I get bored easily. I've been bored most of my life."

Billy Collins (1941–)

U.S. poet laureate whose work is rooted in quotidian experience and who credits boredom as his "muse" and "the mother of creativity."

Boredom is paradise . . . [it's] the blessed absence of what the world offers as "interesting," i.e., the lures of fashion, media and other people, which, you may recall, Sartre considered Hell.

Quentin Crisp (1908–1999)

Flamboyant author of The Naked Civil Servant *(1968) and other autobiographical books filled with wit, candor, and a tinge of ennui.*

You fall out of your mother's womb, you crawl across open country under fire, and drop into your grave.

Nothing in our culture, not even home computers, is more overrated than the epidermal felicity of two featherless bipeds in desperate congress.

My Dinner with André is as boring as being alive.

Lady Honoria Dedlock

Central character in Charles Dickens's Bleak House *(1852) whose marriage to Sir Leicester Dedlock raises her social status but also induces "an exhausted composure, a worn-out placidity, an equanimity of fatigue. . . ."*

My Lady Dedlock (who is childless), looking out in the early twilight from her boudoir at a keeper's lodge, and seeing the light of a fire upon the latticed panes, and smoke rising from the chimney, and a child, chased by a woman, running out into the rain to meet the shining figure of a wrapped-up man coming through the gate, has been put quite out of temper. My Lady Dedlock says she has been "bored to death."

CHARLES DICKENS

Dino

Alienated narrator of Alberto Moravia's Boredom *(La noia; 1960) who defines his own* noia *as "the lack of a relationship with external things" and delineates his condition in the novel's prologue:*

For many people boredom is the opposite of amusement; and amusement means distraction, forgetfulness. For me, boredom is not the opposite of amusement. . . . Boredom to me consists in a kind of insufficiency, or inadequacy, or lack of reality. Reality, when I am bored, has always had the same disconcerting effect on me as (to use a metaphor) a too-short blanket has upon a sleeping man on a winter night: he pulls it down over his feet and his chest gets cold, then he pulls it up to his chest and his feet get cold, and so he never succeeds in falling properly asleep. . . . The feeling of boredom originates for me in a sense of the absurdity of a reality which is insufficient, or anyhow unable, to convince me of its own effective existence.

ALBERTO MORAVIA

Marie Du Deffand (1697–1780)
French noblewoman whose bleak outlook was an acute manifestation of the decadence and

ennui that afflicted the ancien régime. She defined it in a letter to Voltaire in 1759:

All conditions and all circumstances seem equally unfortunate to me, from the angel to the oyster. The grievous thing is to be born.

Duke Jean Floressas des Esseintes

Protagonist of Against the Grain *(À rebours; 1884) by Joris-Karl Huysmans. Weary of the amusements of Paris, the duke resorts to such decadent diversions as having the shell of a tortoise encrusted with jewels.*

Travel . . . struck him [des Esseintes] as being a waste of time, since he believed that the imagination could provide a more-than-adequate substitute for the vulgar reality of actual experience.

J. K. Huysmans

Gustave Flaubert (1821–1880)

French novelist whose Madame Bovary *(1857) is a vivid chronicle of middle-class ennui.*

Madame Bovary, c'est moi.

Deep within me there is a radical, intimate, bitter and incessant *boredom* which prevents me from enjoying anything and which smothers my soul. It reappears at any excuse, just as the swollen corpses of drowned dogs pop to the surface despite the stones that have been tied round their necks.

Goncourt Brothers, Jules (1830–1870) and Edmond (1822–1896)

French novelists and art critics whose works reflect their own ennui and disenchantment. The novelist Anita Brookner described them as "two men who were without illusions, without that euphoria or that tonic energy that would

*have enabled them to bear their melancholia
with a certain amount of philosophy."*

There are moments when, faced with our
lack of success, I wonder whether we
are failures, proud but impotent. One
thing reassures me as to our value: the
boredom that afflicts us. It is the hallmark of quality in modern men.

No cause is worth dying for, any
government can be lived with, nothing
but art may be believed in, and literature
is the only confession.

Graham Greene (1904–1991)
*Prolific British novelist whose fifty-four books
ranged from* The Power and the Glory
(1940) and The Third Man *(1950) to* This
Gun for Hire *(1936) and* Travels With
My Aunt *(1969). Paul Theroux detected in
Greene an "imperious boredom" that led him
to play Russian Roulette as a boy and to travel*

the world as much to court danger and disease as to provide material for his fiction.

While at Ambervale, to escape the "oppression of boredom," he [Greene] walked over the hills to Chesterfield and found a dentist: "I described to him the symptoms, which I knew well, of an abscess."

"He tapped a perfectly good tooth with his little mirror and I reacted in the correct way. 'Better have it out,' he advised."

"'Yes,' I said, 'but with ether.'"

"A few minutes' unconsciousness was like a holiday from the world. I had lost a good tooth, but the boredom was for a time dispersed."

NORMAN SHERRY

Hamlet

Shakespeare's enigmatic Prince of Denmark who is paralyzed by self-analysis and plagued by ennui:

How weary, stale, flat and unprofitable
Seem to me all the uses of the world.

WILLIAM SHAKESPEARE

Ben Hecht (1894–1964)

American playwright, novelist, and screenwriter probably best known as the co-author of The Front Page *(1928) and* Twentieth Century *(1932).*

I can imagine no achievement or praise that could alter the ennui in which I exist, or add the smallest permanent dimension to my life. I have had both success and failure. They were like meals, digested and forgotten.

Sherlock Holmes

Arthur Conan Doyle's brilliant master detective in A Study in Scarlet *(1887) and other novels and short stories, for whom daily life is so dull and unchallenging that he combats between-case ennui by playing the violin and shooting cocaine (though he never actually says, "Quick, Watson, the needle!").*

Nikolai Ivanov

Self-absorbed title character of Anton Chekhov's play whose dissatisfaction with his marriage, anxiety over his debts, and boredom with his provincial neighbors drain his zest for life ("there's a lethargy in my soul," he complains to his doctor). Ivanov's obsessive fear that he spreads boredom ends in tragedy.

Mick Jagger (1943–)

Lead singer of the Rolling Stones and co-author of many of the band's hits, including "(I Can't Get No) Satisfaction."

The real pleasure of being Mick Jagger was in having everything but being tempted by nothing . . . a smoldering ill will which silk clothes, fine food, wine, women, and every conceivable physical pampering somehow aggravated . . . a drained and languorous, exquisitely photogenic ennui.

ANONYMOUS (QUOTED BY PHILIP NORMAN)

Rolling Stone: Jack White told me that when the White Stripes were opening for the Stones, you were rehearsing "Satisfaction" at sound check. Don't you know that one by now?

Mick Jagger: I don't have to work too hard on that one [laughs]. The nice way of thinking about that would be that we're still playing it with enthusiasm.

And if I don't fuck with the ending of that song I get really, really bored—then I have no enthusiasm. I have to fuck with the ending a bit.

RS: Do you get bored?

MJ: You have to find lots of distractions, without turning on the TV. Exploring the local surrounding is the perfect thing, but sometimes I'm too physically tired to do much. You get bored, and that's how you end up doing really stupid things out on the road [laughs]. I think I'm over that now.

Rolling Stone

Franz Kafka (1883–1924)
Czech writer of nightmarish fiction—The Trial (1925), "The Metamorphosis" (1912)—whose name has come to signify absurdity and dread.

I hate everything that does not relate to literature; conversations bore me (even when they relate to literature), to visit people bores me, the joys and sorrows of my relatives bore me to my soul. Conversation takes the importance, the seriousness, the truth out of everything I think.

Philip Larkin (1922–1985)

One of England's greatest modern poets was prey to depression and ennui:

Life is first boredom, then fear.
Whether or not we use it, it goes,
And leaves what something
    hidden from us chose,
And age, and then the only
    end of age.

I suppose I shall become free [of mother] at 60, three years before the cancer starts. What a bloody, sodding awful life.

Marquis de Sade (1740–1814)

French nobleman whose name is synonymous with perversion and cruelty. Imprisoned in the Bastille and the insane asylum at Charenton, he soothed the boredom of incarceration by writing sexually graphic novels and plays.

Dean Martin (1917–1995)

Suave American entertainer who, after his breakup with Jerry Lewis in 1956, became a popular recording, television, and movie star, and a very rich man. He was a favorite with audiences if not always with critics: Time *magazine's Richard Corliss wrote that Martin "radiated stupefaction" on his television show, and* Variety *said of his Las Vegas nightclub act, "Dean Martin, in living ennui, presents a better caricature of himself than any other impressionist."*

Was his nonchalance—which sometimes bordered on somnambulism—inscrutable

*serenity, or terminal ennui? Did he give the
impression he was phoning it in because
he was phoning it in? His biographer Nick
Tosches pronounced him a menefreghista,
one who simply doesn't give a damn.*

*Dean spent his final years as a semirecluse
and once described his daily routine to a
golfing partner:*

It's great. I wake up every morning,
massive bowel movement. The Mexican
maid makes me some breakfast. Down
to the club here. At least nine holes. A
nice lunch. Go home, sit by the TV. The
Mexican maid makes me a nice dinner.
A few drinks, Go to bed. Wake up the
next morning. Another massive bowel
movement. Beautiful. This is my life.

W. Somerset Maugham (1874–1965)
*Popular British author of short stories, novels,
and plays written from a detached, ironic
point of view. He is perhaps best known for*

his semiautobiographical novels, including Of Human Bondage *(1915),* Cakes and Ale *(1930), and* The Summing Up *(1938), in which he limns his prickly brand of ennui:*

My sympathies are limited. I can only be myself, and partly by nature, partly by the circumstances of my life, it is a partial self. I am not a social person. I cannot get drunk and feel a great love for my fellow-men. Convivial amusement has always somewhat bored me. When people sitting in an ale-house or drifting down the river in a boat start singing I am silent. I have never even sung a hymn. I do not much like being touched, and I have always to make a slight effort over myself not to draw away when someone links his arm in mine. I can never forget myself. The hysteria of the world repels me, and I never feel more aloof than when I am in the midst of a throng surrendered to a violent feeling of mirth or sorrow.

Meursault

Aloof protagonist of Albert Camus's The Stranger *(L'etranger; 1942) who is sentenced to death for killing a young Arab on a deserted Algerian beach. The most damning evidence at trial is that he had sent his mother to an old-age home and didn't cry at her funeral. Mersault's real crime is his ennui: Asked by the magistrate whether he is sorry for the murder he replies, "What I felt was less regret than a vague boredom."*

Robert Morley (1908–1992)

Rotund English stage and film actor and master of light comedy whose haughty, slightly fatigued persona was close to reality: During a London run of André Roussin's Hook, Line and Sinker, *Morely had to make an entrance soaking wet after having fallen into a river, upon which Joan Plowright would swoon and drop the tray she was carrying, and Morley would then pick everything up. But at one matinee, as soon as she dropped the tray, Morley, overcome with ennui, said, "You pick them up today, I'm too tired." He also appeared in a series of British Airways commercials in the United States as a passenger who demands (and gets) comfort.*

Arriving in a new place, I am invariably disappointed. This is not how I pictured Samarkand, I tell myself. The truth is, of course, I never pictured it at all. As soon as I arrive, I want to be off. I find the harbor or the bus station, and read the destination boards. If the lettering is indecipherable, so much the better. I hop on the coach and pretend I know where I'm going, pay the conductor the same amount as the man who sits beside me, alight where he alights, and wonder what the hell I'm going to do in a hillside slum for three hours before the bus returns. But I find something, even if its only to sit in the café in the square, and if possible in the sun. I watch nothing whatever happening, and am content. On the way back I grab the seat next to the window and am disappointed that the route is familiar.

Audie Murphy (1924–1971)

Scrawny, baby-faced teenager who became America's most decorated infantryman in World War II. After the parades and testimonials he became a successful movie actor, but couldn't adjust to peacetime: Two failed marriages, addiction to prescription drugs, and compulsive gambling had put him on the verge of bankruptcy when he was killed in a plane crash at the age of forty-six.

War both made and unmade Audie Murphy because, unlike all those veterans who were able to resume their lives and put the days of killing and blood behind them, he was never able to recover from the profound lassitude, the boredom, inscribed upon his inner life.

Don Graham

Allen H. Neuharth (1924–)

Self-made American multimillionaire, author, and founder of USA Today.

Allen H. Neuharth: What do you want to talk about, Frances? Yourself? Me? Both of us?

Frances Lear: I want to know what you're going to do with the rest of your life, and I want to know whether you're bored or not.

Neuharth: Well, I have a very low boring point. My critics say I have a quick temper and a low boiling point, but my boring point is much lower. My remedy for it is to fix whatever I'm doing and get it behind me and go on and do something else. When I have a thing under control, a newspaper like *USA*

Today or a new acquisition or project, as soon as I've got it fixed I want to move on to something else.

Lear: I get bored very quickly too. I always run to do something I've fallen in love with, leaving behind what I've been doing. It's a great problem, but I think people like you and me, if I may include myself with you, are catalysts. I think we make things happen.

Neuharth: I plead guilty to that.

Lear: Do you have friends in the business world who are bored?

Neuharth: I know people who put up with boredom year after year because they're afraid to do anything about it. They may have some idea of what they'd like to do, but they don't have the guts to do it.

Lear's Magazine

Neville
Unfortunate little boy who "died of ennui" in Edward Gorey's Gashlycrumb Tinies.

Profirio Rubirosa (1909–1965)
Legendary playboy whose affairs with and marriages to a series of actresses and socialites made him an international celebrity. He was killed when his Ferrari hit a tree on a Parisian boulevard.

It's one of my fundamental principles: I would prefer risking everything instead of being bored.

George Sanders (1906–1972)
Russian-born British film actor whose cultivated caddishness gave distinction to dozens of mediocre productions. A man of many talents, he was fluent in several languages; played piano, guitar, and saxophone; sang in a rich baritone; and

*was a natural athlete and games player. He
designed houses, built furniture, and was an
amateur electrician who held several patents.
He excelled at mathematics and astronomy
(he built his own telescopes) and dismantled
and rebuilt automobile engines for fun. Yet he
described himself as "boring" and "by vocation
a dilettante." Asked what interested him most
he replied, "sleeping."*

*In 1950, Sanders won the Best Supporting
Actor Oscar for his portrayal of the acerbic
critic Addison De Witt in* All About Eve,
*though he always considered acting beneath
his dignity and did little to further his career.*

Acting is like roller skating. Once
you know how to do it, it is neither
stimulating nor exciting.

Regarding your question as to my
reaction to the prospect of an additional
stay in Spain, I can only tell you that
it makes no difference to me. I have
reached that happy state of being

indifferent to my surroundings. I have liberated myself at long last from morbid concern regarding the terrestrial co-ordinates of my geographical location. This used to be one of my biggest ambivalences. I have successfully resolved it. I live in the mind, which is the only place to look for happiness.

The trips which you suggest I should make, to Segovia, Toledo, etc.; I did all those things years ago. They bore the shit out of me. I employ my time staring into space at the hotel or staring into space at the studio and am perfectly happy.

LETTER TO BRIAN AHERNE, 1958

Dear World: I am leaving because I am bored. I feel I have lived long enough. I am leaving you with your worries in this sweet cesspool. Good luck.

Arthur Schopenhauer (1788–1860)

Reclusive German philosopher for whom ordinary human interaction was excruciatingly boring:

There can be no doubt that to Schopenhauer's mind ennui was an evil every whit as palpable as want. He hated and feared them both with the painful susceptibility of a self-centered man; he strove resolutely from his youth to protect himself against these twin disasters of life. The determined fashion in which he guarded his patrimony from loss resembled the determined fashion in which he strove—with less success—to guard himself from boredom. The vapid talk, the little wearisome iterations, which most of us bear resignedly enough because custom has taught us patience, were to him intolerable afflictions. He retaliated by an ungracious dismissal of society as something pitiably and uniformly contemptible.

Agnes Repplier

Artie Shaw (1910–2004)

Swing Era clarinetist and bandleader who walked away from show business at the height of success because he was bored with fame and couldn't bear to play the same music every night. After brief marriages to a series of glamorous women including Lana Turner and Ava Gardner, he became a writer, dairy farmer, nationally ranked marksman, and expert fly fisherman.

If you wanna dance, a windshield wiper'll do it—all you need is a beat.

Andy Warhol (1927–1987)

American artist and social commentator, he was a rare example of the ennuyé who embraces his boredom:

I like boring things.

Switzerland is my favorite place . . . because it's so—nothing. There's absolutely nothing to do.

Evelyn Waugh (1903–1966)

British writer of satirical novels who suffered lifelong boredom:

He suffered fools not at all, yet boredom frequently—and excruciatingly. Boredom to Waugh was, like a disease, palpable in its effects. In *Work Suspended* he has his narrator say of another character that he was "still smarting with the ruthless boredom of my last two or three meetings with him." "Ruthless boredom" is a juxtaposition only an acute sufferer could contrive.

Joseph Epstein

WHEREVER YOU GO, THERE YOU ARE!

In every moment, we find ourselves at the crossroads of here and now. It often seems as if we are preoccupied with . . . a future that hasn't arrived yet. We look for some place else to stand, where we hope things will be better.

JON KABAT-ZINN

For most of our marriage, I've been accused of being a person who could never take a vacation. No: "A picture of distraction," apparently, was I.

In my early freelance-writing years, Ben claimed you could never get me *away* from my desk, where I tended to wait, eyes wide, every tendon straining, for the phone *not* to ring. *Then*, once *on* actual vacation, I was apparently a person who was never . . . *in* the Moment. No, apparently I was the sort of person who was always bringing books and tapes and notebooks and laptops and other junk with which to *shield* myself from the Moment.

The theory was freely proffered that I was a person who *feared* the Moment.

And between you and me, maybe it's true. . . .

Because let's admit, in life as we know it, the Moment is often *much* less than advertised.

Waterskiing, for instance. This is not about waterskiing. It is taking a bumpy car ride to the dock to pick up gear. Strapping oneself into a smelly vest. Sitting on a bench near barrels of oil and gull poop, waiting for others to strap themselves into their vests, to make sure they get the really *good* vests, the really *snug* vests—

Do you know what I mean? It's never about the forty seconds of sheer terror while actually *on* the water skis.

The fact is, so *little* of life is actually spent in the Moment. No, most of the time we find ourselves dog-paddling through all the interstitial stuff *preparing* for the moment. Because at its core, the human condition is not to *star* in the Moment, but to basically work in the *production* crew on the *set* of the *Moment*. You know? The sixty-second Thanksgiving toast will be performed at 8:33. But in the meantime, grocery bags need to be carried in, carrots peeled, water glasses filled. . . . All that enervating, lifeblood-draining *preparation* that makes one feel so much *less* alive than if one were slumped in a hammock with a vodka cranberry rereading *Valley of the Dolls*.

However, as I trundle ever deeper into the echoing canyons of my thirties, I feel a sea change coming on. I feel myself in the grip of a burnished new wisdom. I find myself more and more able to strip away the layers of fear . . . the fear of being bored.

SANDRA TSING LOH

It is not irritating to be where one is. It is only irritating to think one would like to be somewhere else.

JOHN CAGE

"IS THAT ALL THERE IS?"

WORDS AND MUSIC BY JERRY LEIBER AND MIKE STOLLER

(Spoken) I remember when I was a very little girl, our house caught on fire. I'll never forget the look on my father's face as he gathered me up in his arms and raced through the burning building out to the pavement. I stood there shivering in my pajamas and watched the whole world go up in flames. And when it was all over I said to myself, "Is that all there is to a fire?"

(Sung) Is that all there is, is that all there is?
If that's all there is my friends, then let's keep dancing.
Let's break out the booze and have a ball,
If that's all there is.

(Spoken) And when I was twelve years old, my father took me to a circus, the greatest show on earth. There were clowns and elephants and dancing bears, and a beautiful lady in pink tights flew high above our heads. And so I sat there watching the marvelous spectacle. I had the feeling that something was missing. I don't know what, but when it was over, I said to myself, "Is that all there is to a circus?"

(Sung) Is that all there is, is that all there is?
If that's all there is my friends, then let's keep dancing.
Let's break out the booze and have a ball,
If that's all there is.

(Spoken) Then I fell in love, head over heels in love, with the most wonderful boy in the world. We would take long walks by the river or just sit for hours gazing into each other's eyes. We were so very much in love. Then one day he went away and I thought I'd die, but I didn't, and when I didn't I said to myself, "Is that all there is to love?"

(Sung) Is that all there is, is that all there is?
If that's all there is my friends, then let's keep dancing.

(Spoken) I know what you must be saying to your-selves: if that's the way she feels about it why doesn't she just end it all? Oh, no, not me. I'm in no hurry for that final disappointment, for I know just as well as I'm standing here talking to you, when that final moment comes and I'm breathing my last breath, I'll be saying to myself . . .

(Sung) Is that all there is, is that all there is?
If that's all there is my friends, then let's keep dancing.
Let's break out the booze and have a ball,
If that's all there is.

SELECT BIBLIOGRAPHY

Adams, Henry. *The Education of Henry Adams.* New York: Modern Library, 1999.

————. *Selected Letters.* Cambridge, MA: Harvard University Press, 1992.

Aherne, Brian. *A Dreadful Man.* New York: Simon and Schuster, 1979.

Arlen, Michael. *The Green Hat.* New York: George H. Doran, 1924.

Bangs, John Kendrick. *A Hint to Virtue.* New York: Harper & Brothers, 1894.

Barnes, Julian. *Staring at the Sun.* New York: Harper and Row, 1988.

Barthelme, Frederick, and Steven Barthelme. *Double Down.* Boston: Houghton Mifflin, 1999.

Barthes, Roland. *The Grain of the Voice.* New York: Hill and Wang, 1985.

Bateson, Mary Catherine. *Peripheral Visions: Learning Along the Way.* New York: HarperCollins, 1994.

Baudelaire, Charles. *The Flowers of Evil.* New York: Oxford University Press, 1998.

Beckett, Samuel. *Endgame.* New York: Grove Press, 1992.

————. *Waiting for Godot.* London: Faber and Faber, 1955.

Bellow, Saul. *Humboldt's Gift.* New York: Penguin, 1996.

Bennett, Alan. *Writing Home.* New York: Random House, 1994.

Bernanos, George. *The Diary of a Country Priest.* New York: Delta, 1956.

Berryman, John. "Dream Song 14." In *Short Poems.* New York: Farrar, Straus & Giroux, 1967.

Bierce, Ambrose. *The Devil's Dictionary.* New York: Oxford University Press, 1999.

Blakey, Nancy H. "Boredom: The Cauldron of Creativity." *Mothering*, July–August 2001.

Bodett, Tom. "Wait Divisions." In *Small Comforts.* Reading, MA: Addison-Wesley, 1987.

Boorstin, Daniel. *The Image; Or, What Happened to the American Dream.* New York: Atheneum, 1962.

Boswell, James. *The Journals of James Boswell.* New Haven: Yale University Press, 1991.

Brodsky, Joseph. "In Praise of Boredom." In *On Grief and Reason.* New York: Farrar, Straus & Giroux, 1995.

Brookner, Anita. *Brief Lives.* New York: Vintage, 1992.

————. *Falling Slowly.* New York: Vintage, 1998.

————. *Romanticism and Its Discontents.* New York: Farrar, Straus & Giroux, 2000.

Byron, George Gordon. *Lord Byron, the Major Works.* New York: Oxford University Press, 2000.

Camus, Albert. *The Fall.* New York: Vintage, 1991.

————. *The Plague.* New York: Vintage, 1991.

————. *The Stranger.* New York: Knopf, 1993.

Caruba, Alan. *Boring Stuff: How to Spot It, How to Avoid It.* Maplewood, NJ: Boring Institute, 1987.

Cervantes Saavedra, Miguel de. *Don Quixote.* New York: Ecco, 2003.

Chandler, Raymond. *Selected Letters of Raymond Chandler.* New York: Columbia University Press, 1981.

Cheever, Susan. "Wake Me When It's Over, Grads." *Newsday*, May 26, 2004.

Chekhov, Anton. *The Plays of Anton Chekhov.* New York: HarperCollins, 1997.

Collier, Richard. *The Rainbow People.* New York: Dodd, Mead, 1984.

Connolly, Cyril. *The Unquiet Grave.* New York: Harper & Brothers, 1945.

Conrad, Joseph. *The Mirror of the Sea.* London: Methuen, 1906.

Cooley, Mason. *City Aphorisms.* New York: AMS, 1990.

Coupland, Douglas. *Generation X.* New York: St. Martin's, 1991.

————. *Life After God.* New York: Pocket Books, 1994.

Craveri, Benedetta. *Madame du Deffand and Her World.* Boston: Godine, 1994.

Crisp, Quentin. *The Naked Civil Servant*. New York: Penguin, 1997.

Csikszentmihalyi, Mihaly. *Beyond Boredom and Anxiety*. San Francisco: Jossey-Bass, 2000.

————. *Finding Flow*. New York: Basic Books, 1997.

Csikszentmihalyi, Mihaly, and Jeremy Hunter. "The Positive Psychology of Interested Adolescents." *Journal of Youth and Adolescence* (February 2003).

Dickens, Charles. *Bleak House*. New York: Knopf, 1991.

Dobbs, Michael. *House of Cards*. New York: HarperPaperbacks, 1990.

Dostoyevsky, Fyodor. *Notes from the Underground*. New York: Norton, 2001.

Duany, Andres, Elizabeth Plater-Zyberk, and Jeff Speck. *Suburban Nation: The Rise of Sprawl and the Decline of the American Dream*. New York: North Point, 2000.

Dumas, Alexandre. *The Three Musketeers*. New York: Modern Library, 1999.

Edgeworth, Maria. *Ennui*. New York: Penguin, 1992.

Edmunson, Mark. *Why Read?* New York: Bloomsbury, 2004.

Eliot, T. S. "The Love Song of J. Alfred Prufrock." In *The Waste Land, Prufrock, and Other Poems*. Mineola, NY: Dover, 1998.

Emerson, Ralph Waldo. *The Essential Writings of Ralph Waldo Emerson*. New York: Modern Library, 2000.

————. *The Portable Emerson*. New York: Penguin, 1981.

Epstein, Joseph. "The Outrageous Mr. Wu." In *Partial Payments*. New York: Norton, 1989.

Epstein, Norrie. *The Friendly Dickens*. New York: Viking Penguin, 1998.

Fadiman, Clifton. *Reading I've Liked*. New York: Simon and Schuster, 1941.

Fenichel, Otto. "The Psychology of Boredom." In *Collected Papers*. New York: Norton, 1953.

Ferrell, Jeff. "Boredom, Crime and Criminology." *Theoretical Criminology* 8 (2004).

Flaubert, Gustave. *Madame Bovary*. Oxford: Oxford University Press, 1999.

Fox, James. *White Mischief*. New York: Random House, 1982.

Frankl, Viktor. *The Will to Meaning*. New York: New American Library, 1969.

Fromm, Erich. "Affluence and Ennui in Our Society." In *For the Love of Life*. New York: Free Press, 1985.

————. *The Sane Society*. New York: Henry Holt, 1990.

Fussell, Paul. *The Anti-Egotist*. New York: Oxford University Press, 1994.

————. *Wartime*. New York: Oxford University Press, 1989.

Gilbert, W. S., and Arthur Sullivan. *The Complete Plays of Gilbert and Sullivan*. New York: Doubleday, 1984.

Goldberg, M. Hirsh. *The Complete Book of Greed*. New York: William Morrow, 1994.

Gooding, Judson. "How to Cope with Boredom." *Reader's Digest*, February 1976.

Graham, Don. *No Name on the Bullet: A Biography of Audie Murphy*. New York: Viking, 1989.

Halberstam, David. *The Best and the Brightest*. New York: Random House, 1972.

Halpern, Daniel. *Our Private Lives*. Hopewell, NJ: Ecco Press, 1998.

Harris, Mark. *Bang the Drum Slowly*. New York: Knopf, 1956.

Harrison, Jim. "A Really Big Lunch." *New Yorker*, September 6, 2004.

Hart, Moss. *Act One*. New York: Random House, 1959.

Healy, Seán Desmond. *Boredom, Self and Culture*. London: Associated University Presses, 1984.

Hecht, Ben. *A Child of the Century*. New York: Simon and Schuster, 1954.

Heidegger, Martin. *Existence and Being*. Chicago: Regnery, 1949.

Horsley, Sebastian. "The Brothel Creeper." *Observer*, September 19, 2004.

Hugo, Victor. *Thoughts*. New York: Funk and Wagnalls, 1907.

Huysmans, J. K. *Against Nature*. New York: Penguin, 2003.

Inge, William Ralph. *Lay Thoughts of a Dean.* New York: Putnam, 1926.

Jakob, Michel. "Wakefulness and Obsession: An Interview with E. M. Cioran." *Salmagundi* (Summer 1994).

Jefferson, Thomas. *The Family Letters of Thomas Jefferson.* Columbia, MO: University of Missouri Press, 1966.

Johnson, Samuel. *The Letters of Samuel Johnson.* Princeton: Princeton University Press, 1992–1994.

Kabat-Zinn, Jon. *Wherever You Go There You Are.* New York: Hyperion, 1994.

Kapuscinski, Ryszard. *The Soccer War.* London: Granta, 1990.

Kessler, Lauren. "Dancing With Rose: A Strangely Beautiful Encounter With Alzheimer's Patients Provides Insights That Challenge the Way We View the Disease." *Los Angeles Times Magazine*, August 22, 2004.

Kierkegaard, Søren. *Either/Or.* Princeton: Princeton University Press, 1944.

Knapp, Michael G. "A World War I Retrospective." *Prologue* (Spring 1992).

Kraus, Karl. *No Compromise: Selected Writings of Karl Kraus.* New York: Ungar, 1977.

Kuhn, Reinhard. *The Demon of Noontide: Ennui in Western Literature.* Princeton: Princeton University Press, 1976.

Lapham, Lewis H. *Money and Class in America.* New York: Weidenfeld & Nicolson, 1988.

La Rochefoucauld, [François]. *Maxims.* New York: Penguin, 1959.

Lefcourt, Peter. *The Deal.* New York: Random House, 1991.

Lewis, Sinclair. *Babbitt.* New York: Penguin, 1996.

Linnéa, Sharon. "The New Epidemic: Why We're Bored and What We Can Do About It." www.sharonlinnea.com.

Linton, Ralph. *The Study of Man.* New York: Appleton-Century, 1936.

Lin Yutang. *The Importance of Living.* New York: William Morrow, 1996.

Loh, Sandra Tsing. *A Year in Van Nuys.* New York: Crown, 2001.

Manzoni, Alessandro. *The Betrothed.* New York: Dutton, 1956.

Maugham, W. Somerset. *The Moon and Sixpence.* New York: Arno, 1977.

————. *The Summing Up.* New York: Doubleday, 1938.

May, Rollo. *The Discovery of Being: Writings in Existential Psychology.* New York: Norton, 1983.

McLaughlin, Mignon. *The Second Neurotic's Notebook.* Indianapolis: Bobbs-Merrill, 1966.

Mencken, Henry Louis. *Minority Report: H. L. Mencken's Notebooks.* Baltimore: Johns Hopkins University Press, 1997.

————. *Newspaper Days, 1899–1906.* Baltimore: Johns Hopkins University Press, 1996.

Miller, Arthur. "The Bored and the Violent." In *Echoes Down the Corridor: Collected Essays 1944–2000.* New York: Penguin, 2000.

Mitford, Nancy. *A Talent to Annoy.* New York: Beaufort, 1987.

Moravia, Alberto. *Boredom.* New York: NYRB, 1999.

Moynahan, Brian. *Rasputin: The Saint Who Sinned.* New York: Random House, 1997.

Mumford, Lewis. *The Pentagon of Power.* New York: Harcourt Brace Jovanovich, 1964.

Nietzsche, Friedrich Wilhelm. *Beyond Good and Evil.* New York: Vintage, 1966.

————. *The Gay Science.* New York: Vintage, 1974.

Nisbet, Robert. "Boredom." *Commentary* (September 1982).

————. *Prejudices: A Philosophical Dictionary.* Cambridge, MA: Harvard University Press, 1982.

Norman, Philip. *The Life and Good Times of the Rolling Stones.* New York: Harmony, 1989.

Ogden, Howard. *Pensamentoes, Volume II.* Los Angeles: Potshot Press, 2004.

Oppenheim, E. Phillips. *The Malefactor.* Boston: Little, Brown, 1906.

Ott, Bill. "Fighting Vainly the Old Ennui." *Booklist,* May 15, 2001.

Parker, Dorothy. *The Portable Dorothy Parker.* New York: Viking, 1973.

Pascal, Blaise. *Pensées.* 1670. New York: Penguin, 1966.

Perelman, S. J. *Eastward Ha!* Short Hills, NJ: Burford, 1998.

Phillips, Adam. *On Kissing, Tickling and Being Bored.* Cambridge: Harvard University Press, 1993.

Phillips, William. *A Sense of the Present.* New York: Chilmark, 1967.

Pound, Ezra. *ABC of Reading.* New York: New Directions, 1987.

Powers, Katherine A. "A Reading Life." *Boston Globe,* July 13, 2003.

Quick, Amanda. *With This Ring.* New York: Bantam, 1998.

Quindlen, Anna. "Doing Nothing is Something." In *Loud and Clear.* New York: Random House, 2004.

Repplier, Agnes. "Ennui." In *Essays in Idleness.* Boston: Houghton Mifflin, 1893.

Resko, John. *Reprieve: The Testament of John Resko.* New York: Doubleday, 1956.

Rivenburg, Roy. "Monotony (Yawn) Could Be the Best Cure for Boredom." *Los Angeles Times,* April 14, 2003.

Rosen, Gerald. *Zen in the Art of J. D. Salinger.* Berkeley: Creative Arts, 1977.

Roth, Philip. *The Ghost Writer.* New York: Vintage, 1995.

Russell, Bertrand. *The Conquest of Happiness.* New York: Liveright, 1996.

Sanders, George. *Memoirs of a Professional Cad.* New York: Putnam, 1960.

Schachtel, Ernest. *Metamorphosis.* New York: Basic Books, 1959.

Schwartz, Lynne Sharon. *Ruined by Reading.* Boston: Beacon Press, 1996.

Sherry, Norman. *The Life of Graham Greene, Volume One: 1904– 1939.* New York: Viking, 1989.

Sibley, Celestine. "Boredom's Fascinating, Readers Say." *Atlanta Constitution,* March 17, 1999.

Spacks, Patricia Meyer. *Boredom: The Literary History of a State of Mind.* Chicago: University of Chicago Press, 1995.

———. "Women and Boredom: The Two Emmas." *Yale Journal of Criticism* (Spring 1989).

Stendhal [Marie Henri Beyle]. *The Red and the Black.* New York: Modern Library, 2003.

Stevens, Wallace. *Notes Toward a Supreme Fiction.* Cummington, MA: Cummington Press, 1942.

Szasz, Thomas. *The Meaning of Mind: Language, Morality, and Neuroscience.* Westport, CT: Praeger, 1996.

Taylor, Bert Leston. *The Charlatans.* Indianapolis: Bobbs-Merrill, 1906.

Thomas, Elizabeth Marshall. *The Hidden Life of Dogs.* Boston: Houghton Mifflin, 1993.

Thoreau, Henry David. *The Writings of Henry David Thoreau.* Boston: Houghton Mifflin, 1906.

Tolstoy, Leo. *Anna Karenina.* New York: Viking, 2001.

Tosches, Nick. *Dino: Living High in the Dirty Business of Dreams.* New York: Doubleday, 1992.

Tynan, Kenneth. *Tynan Right and Left.* New York: Atheneum, 1967.

Updike, John. *Assorted Prose.* New York: Knopf, 1965.

————. *The Coup.* New York: Knopf, 1978.

————. *Self-Consciousness.* New York: Knopf, 1989.

Vidal, Gore. *Palimpsest: A Memoir.* New York: Random House, 1995.

Voltaire [François Marie Arouet]. *Candide.* New York: Modern Library, 2002.

Wilbur, Richard. "Lying." In *Responses: Prose Pieces, 1953–1976.* Ashland, OR: Story Line Press, 2000.

Wilde, Oscar. *A Woman of No Importance.* London: Methuen Drama, 1994.

Winn, Steven. "We Try Our Best to Avoid It, But Boredom Has Its Benefits." *San Francisco Chronicle*, April 2, 2004.

Winter, Richard. *Still Bored in a Culture of Entertainment.* Downers Grove, IL: InterVarsity, 2002.

Zolla, Elemire. *The Eclipse of the Intellectual.* New York: Funk, 1968.

INDEX

ABOUT THE AUTHOR

Jon Winokur is well situated to author a book about ennui, having lived in Southern California for most of his life.